In Defense
of
Read-Aloud

In Defense
of
Read-Aloud
Sustaining Best Practice

STEVEN L. LAYNE
Foreword by Regie Routman

Stenhouse Publishers

Portland, Maine

Stenhouse Publishers
www.stenhouse.com

Library of Congress Cataloging-in-Publication Data
Layne, Steven L.
    In Defense of Read-Aloud: Sustaining Best Practice / Steven L. Layne ; foreword by Regie Routman.
        pages cm
    Includes bibliographical references and index.
    ISBN 978-1-62531-040-8 (pbk.: alk. paper) ISBN 978-1-62531-042-2 (ebook)
    1. Oral reading. I. Title.
    LB1573.5.L39 2015
    372.45'2—dc23
                                        2014032275

Cover and interior design by Lucian Burg, Lu Design Studios, Portland, ME
www.ludesignstudios.com

Manufactured in the United States of America

PRINTED ON 30% PCW
RECYCLED PAPER

21 20 19 18 17 16 15   9 8 7 6 5 4 3 2

DEDICATION

For Lindsay Allen,

a leader who makes me believe.

Never change.

And for the faculty, the staff, and the students of

Southbury Elementary School in Oswego, Illinois.

You make school . . . a dream come true.

CONTENTS

FOREWORD

Teachers have been reading aloud to kids for years—sporadically, enthusiastically, and selectively, but not always as effectively and joyfully as possible. Prolific author and esteemed educator Steven Layne re-envisions read-aloud by bringing the process to a showstopping performance that leaves students of all ages engaged, transfixed, and begging for more. Best of all, he shows us exactly how we, too, can become highly skilled in reading aloud great books we love.

In Defense of Read-Aloud is grounded in solid, extensive research that definitively shows the positive effect of reading aloud on student engagement, thinking, and reading achievement. Including a history of reading aloud backed up not just by solid research but also by the wide experiences of notable educators and authors, we learn how and why reading aloud is best practice and beneficial at every grade level. Writing in a conversational tone that is at times serious, at times humorous, and at times a call to action, Steven convinces us that reading aloud must be a cornerstone of every teaching day regardless of the age level, subject matter, or discipline we teach.

Steven is a seasoned performer, and he applies his well-honed craft to teach us how to perform a highly effective read-aloud. He shares his secrets and tips for ensuring that every read-aloud is a surefire success that has listeners on the edge of their seats. I know that feeling. I experienced that revelation of total engagement and awe the first time I heard Steven speak. It was in 2012, at the annual conference of the International Literacy Association in Chicago. I arrived more than an hour before his general session so I could wish him good luck and meet his family. (Steven and I had met just once before—more about that later—but I'd never had the opportunity to hear him speak.) Much to my surprise, ropes cordoned off the front hall of the huge convention center venue, and no amount of sweet-talking the "guards" convinced them I should be allowed entry. I should have figured out right then that Steven was a rock star.

When I heard him speak, I was riveted, drawn in to his ideas in a way I've never forgotten. In his well-honed and well-known "Balcony People" address, he took note of all the people in his life who have supported his efforts, those people in the metaphorical balcony who have been there for him to contribute to the successful educator, author, and person he is today. Steven doesn't deliver a typical presentation. He tells stories with great power, emotion, and action. He uses every part of his being and humanness to reel us in, and once hooked, we are with him totally. We are literally on the edge of our seats. His voice ranges from a whisper to a shout, from a suggestion to a command. He is convincing! We are mesmerized and transformed. We trust what he is telling us.

Steven works the same magic in *In Defense of Read-Aloud*. He tells us "there is an 'art' to performing a read-aloud well" (91). We learn how to deliver a great read-aloud, prepare for it, and adjust our voice while reading. He elaborates on reading aloud with appropriate expression, phrasing, pace, inflection, volume, enunciation, tone, and pitch—all of which cue the listener and the reader in to the character and the author's intention.

To further work the read-aloud magic on our students, Steven urges us to become knowledgeable literacy leaders who promote reading aloud, see it as valuable instructional time, and ensure that it is no longer "marginalized" in our schools. We are advised to become "intentional and strategic" and go beyond just oral reading. Reading aloud well is hard work that requires a commitment and excellent preparation, but the payoff is huge.

To ensure we read aloud successfully, Steven provides practical read-aloud guidelines such as these:

- Become familiar with the book before reading it.

- Launch the book successfully.

- Provide a purpose for listening.

- Work out an advantageous seating arrangement.

- Plan stopping points: "Every stopping point is a secret reading-skill-reinforcement lesson just waiting to happen" (34).

- Teach reading skills such as visualization, inferring, and sequencing.

- Plan strategically for the end of the read-aloud.

- Work out a positive solution for those students who get the book and read ahead.

- Choose and balance the books and genres we read aloud.

Several unique features of the book also provide additional guidelines and advice. There are position statements from prominent educators on what they believe about the importance of reading aloud and why. There are FAQs—frequently asked questions—in a "Dear Steven" format that he answers with wisdom, grace, and much humor. And there are classroom letters to authors such as Lois Lowry, Katherine Paterson, Nancy Werlin, and Andrew Clements and their exceedingly thoughtful responses that provide insight into how and why authors write and where they get their ideas.

Perhaps most valuable of all are all the wonderful and extensive read-aloud recommendations for grades K–12. Favorite titles and descriptions of "books we love to read aloud" come from distinguished classroom teachers, teacher-librarians, and well-known "literacy stars" such as Donalyn Miller, Kelly Gallagher, Penny Kittle, and Linda Hoyt, to name a few—and, of course, we get Steven's favorites. We learn about favorite picture books, chapter books, fiction, and nonfiction titles, including resources to help us find notable nonfiction read-alouds. Steven also shares his five favorite nonfiction read-alouds for grades K–3, 4–6, 7–9, and 10–12.

In addition, advantages to reading aloud are dispersed throughout the book, and there are many. We and our students have the opportunity to

- become hooked on a book and want to read and reread it;

- change our attitudes about books and reading;

- listen to and comprehend a book on a significantly higher level than if we were reading silently;

- foster a love of reading;

- understand characters better, including ourselves;

- go beyond stereotypes and become more tolerant of differences in the world;

- become part of a thoughtful classroom community through the deep reflection and discussion a great read-aloud can promote; and

- value the role of stories in our lives.

It was a story, in fact, that cemented my friendship with Steven. We first met in Georgia, in the heat of the summer of 2011, where we were both speakers at a literacy conference. We happened to sit next to each other at a dinner graciously hosted by the conference organizers. There were more than a dozen other people at that dinner, but we connected on such a deep literary and human level that we barely spoke to the others. In the course of our conversation, Steven told me a startling story (as only he could tell it—with great drama and humor) of not getting picked up that afternoon by the limousine driver "Victor," who was supposed to be waiting at the airport for him. Although a frustrated Steven reaches Victor on his cell phone, Victor is curt and says someone else will come to the airport. That someone else eventually shows up and drives Steven to a seedy part of town where he is then transferred to another car and driver—twice! All the while, a worried-for-his-safety Steven continues to call Victor, who stops answering the phone. Then it hits me. All the time that Steve was in uncertain transit, Victor was transporting *me*—driving on the freeway above the speed limit and weaving all over the place while talking on the phone—to Steven! I had feared for my own safety, and the only reason Victor stopped answering his phone was that I demanded he do so. It was a harrowing experience for both Steven and me, one that we can laugh about today. And, like any good story that is intimately shared, it connected us in a personal, heartfelt way.

Since that time, Steven and I have kept in touch, and at his invitation I had the pleasure of speaking at Judson University for an all-day literacy and leadership workshop. The evening before the workshop, we enjoyed a "heart-and-mind" dinner together where we savored rich conversations on a variety of topics connected to literacy, leadership, and life. I also got to meet Steven's faculty, graduate students, and family. I saw firsthand how well loved and appreciated he is and what an amazing contribution he continues to make toward literacy and learning at all levels.

In Defense of Read-Aloud is another terrific contribution to literacy; it will persuade you to make reading aloud a daily priority, to see it as crucial instructional time, and to never leave it out. This book will also leave you motivated to read! I was so inspired by a sixth-grade teacher's letter to author Ben Mikaelsen and Ben's response about *Touching*

Spirit Bear that I felt *compelled* to immediately get the novel. I read it in one sitting where I savored the stirring, harrowing, beautifully crafted story. Reading the book caused me to reflect deeply on the power of anger, love, and forgiveness—in the toughest of circumstances. I felt enriched when I finished that book. I wanted everyone to know about it.

Steven Layne's thoughtful book concludes with his twelve favorite read-alouds. Two especially stand out for me. One is Steven's own first novel for teens, the acclaimed *This Side of Paradise*, which he includes because of all the affirming letters he's received from teachers over the years describing its powerful effect on their students. The second is *Stargirl* by Jerry Spinelli, which is one of my all-time favorites as well. Steven still reads it aloud to his graduate students. I felt immediately compelled to reread it because of what Steven wrote:

> The story is timeless; the issues it raises always pertinent. The characters make me look harder at myself than characters from any other piece of fiction that I have ever read. I feel like a better person each time I read the final page—and that has to mean something. (149)

For some of our students, reading aloud may be the only way they will have the opportunity to experience and notice various writing styles, authors' craft, a wide range of genres, and information they might not read on their own, and to reflect on what a particular book means for them. A well-told and well-written story, be it fiction, nonfiction, or poetry, has the power to increase our ability to empathize with others, expand our vision of the world, encourage us to become our best selves, and enrich our hearts and minds. Outstanding authors provide the words, but we can bring those words to life for all students through reading aloud to them. That precious gift means a lot. It is, in fact, priceless.

Regie Routman

ACKNOWLEDGMENTS

Here I am again, writing a K–12 book when a lot of people don't write K–12 books. At least that's what I was told when I started into this business of professional writing. I heard I should write a 4–12 book or a K–5 book or a K–8 book. How about a 6–12 book? Not a K–12 book; it's usually too big a stretch, I was told. I was faced with this dilemma in my first professional book, and I was back in the same place with this one. What I want to talk about applies across all of the grade levels—all of them— and I'm not going to do an elementary version and a secondary version, because if I do that, I'll just be writing the same book all over again with a handful of new examples. So this is it; it's the only one you're going to get, and guess what? It's K–12. It could even be, dare I suggest it, that we need to be doing a lot more talking about K–12 than we do; that's my thought.

Now, it's not only a K–12 book because I say so or because the Stenhouse catalog says so; it's a K–12 book because the voices of some amazing middle and high school teachers have made their way into this book—along with "secondary-ish" colleagues from the trade and professional book industries such as Doug Fisher, Kelly Gallagher, Donalyn Miller, Ben Mikaelsen, and Nancy Werlin. They have been joined by a group of sensational primary and intermediate educators who have joined their voices with those of Ellin Oliver Keene, Maria Walther, Debbie Diller, Katherine Paterson, Andrew Clements, and Lois Lowry.

And if that's not enough (as you will see in Chapter 1), I'll refer to the work of some highly respected researchers and master practitioners who cross all of these grade levels, such as Janet Allen, Nancie Atwell, Isabel Beck, Kylene Beers, Nancy Frey, Gay

Ivey, Stephen Krashen, Teri Lesesne, Lea McGee, Margaret McKeown, Regie Routman, Barbara Samuels, Patrick Shannon, and Jim Trelease.

If all of those voices combined with mine (plus the fact that the content of the book is applicable across every grade level) are not enough to make this a K–12 book, then it's some other kind of book masquerading as a K–12 book. You figure it out and get back to me on that. I'll be in my beach chair just outside my fictitious condo in Hawaii during the cold Chicago winters in case locating me at that time of year is troublesome.

I am often asked why it takes me so long to write a book. There are many reasons such as a large family with whom I spend a great deal of my time, a university job that I love (I work with the most amazing team of faculty, graduate students, and doctoral candidates with whom any person could ever hope to spend time), my travel and speaking obligations, and my service work. Then, there is the fact that I am slow. Horribly, abominably slow. And, I break all of the conventional rules of writing a book, which slows me down even more. I revise sections when I should be drafting others, and I edit sections when I should be revising others. I put off the hardest parts until later and go have a raspberry iced tea with someone fun.

In addition to all of that, when I want to make a strong point (one hopes if you are writing an entire book that there is a fairly robust point to be made), I enlist other voices alongside my own. It is important to me that voices I respect and voices I believe my readers respect (Rita Bean, Brian Cambourne, Henrietta Dombey, Bernadette Dwyer, Linda Gambrell, Jerry Johns, Shelley Stagg Peterson, and Bill Teale) be heard in these pages, because I just know that when we stand shoulder to shoulder on important issues, it will be much more difficult for our message to be ignored. And that, dear reader, takes a lot of time, energy, and coordination, because all of those voices come from people who have a lot on their to-do lists just like you, and it becomes my job to coordinate their lives to include time to contribute to this book.

My thanks to each and every contributor—they've helped make it so much more than it could ever be with my solitary voice. There are no words to express the level of appreciation and devotion I feel toward every employee at Stenhouse for their patience, their professionalism, and the gracious manner in which they conduct themselves at all times. In particular, a shout-out to Chandra Lowe, who helps me get where I need to go sometimes and to my forever friend and editor Bill Varner, who knows how to move me forward and who trusts my ideas. Whenever I hear the song "Hopelessly Devoted to

Acknowledgments

You," I think of my wife, Debbie—and then of Bill Varner.

My literacy family at Judson University in Elgin, Illinois, represents my second family, and they have filled my balcony to overflowing. They are a daily support to all of my work and renew my faith in the education system when I need it most. Last but never least, gratitude to my first family, both nuclear and extended, who cheer me on, endure my absences (or my visits), listen to my ideas . . . and express their faith in my writing. To God be the glory, great things He has done; anything I have accomplished has been done via His gifts and blessings.

Onward!
Steven

CHAPTER 1

What's All the Fuss About Reading Aloud?

Dear Katherine Paterson,

It is with the utmost admiration for the work in your novel *Bridge to Terabithia* that I am writing this letter to you. It has affected my teaching and the students' learning in countless ways that would be nearly impossible to convey in one letter. That being said, however, I feel it is my obligation to let you know the difference you have made in so many lives by writing a novel filled with relatable issues faced in adolescence, and to offer my most sincere gratitude.

As a teacher for more than twenty-five years, educating students in third through fifth grades, I have read hundreds of children's books. I have seen educational trends in teaching literacy come full circle, from the whole-language approach, to small-group differentiation, and everything in between. Your novel *Bridge*, as I lovingly call it, has withstood the test of time more than any other book I have found, and it is a fundamental springboard in my classroom for teaching life lessons. It is the strength of your life messages through the amazing characters that keeps this book timeless.

The development of your characters in *Bridge to Terabithia* ignites deep, real-life connections for readers and acts as a platform upon which to build authentic classroom discussions during read-aloud. Students can relate to both Jess and Leslie as kids seeking to find where they "fit" in their family and in societal norms. No other book addresses sexist stereotypes and parental expectations in such a realistic manner. Leslie's androgynous features; her open relationship with her parents, Bill and Judy; and her incredible imagination make her a real gift to Jess's development. I love that she isn't a typical "girly-girl" worrying about how to dress or what others think. Readers discover through Leslie's actions that succumbing to peer pressure is not necessary to build strong friendships. This is in marked contrast to the view of peer relationships played out in Jess's older sisters Ellie and Brenda, which, again, allows for meaningful dialogue in the classroom.

The theme woven throughout the novel strongly encourages the development of acceptance and tolerance of differences in our world. This brings me to a question that plagues me every time I read *Bridge*, which has been well over twenty times. As I am a product of growing up in the 1970s and being raised by a single mom (which was not nearly the norm), the album *Free to Be You and Me* was a staple in our home. The lyrics sung by Miss Julia Edmunds in your book seem quite a deliberate choice, and they mirror the plot beautifully. I am incredibly curious to know what came first: the idea for the story, inspired perhaps by life experiences, or the lyrics from the album presenting as an idea for this novel?

From the bottom of my heart, I thank you for writing *Bridge to Terabithia*. It is truly a classic. I am so excited to learn all about the background of and inspiration for the story.

Sincerely,
Elizabeth Sompolski

Grade Three
Brook Forest Elementary School
Oak Brook, Illinois

Dear Mrs. Sompolski,

Wow. What a letter. Teachers are my heroes, and a letter from you who have been in the trenches through fad and fiat is more gratifying than I can say.

You asked about the inspiration for Bridge to Terabithia. *I wrote the book in 1975–76 in response to two crises in our family life. The first was my own bout with cancer, which made my children fear that I was going to die, and the second, more tragic event, the death by lightning of our son David's closest friend, Lisa Hill. In many ways Lisa, though only eight when she was killed, was a model for Leslie Burke—the bright, imaginative, funny tomboy. Her sudden, terrible death was a shock to us all but devastating for David. I don't think he will ever fully recover from it, but writing the screenplay and helping produce the movie was very healing for him over thirty years later.*

One thing he told me in the middle of his intense grief was that he and Lisa used to sit by themselves in the corner of the room during music class and sing "'Free to Be You and Me'—real loud." (Apparently, having a best friend of the opposite sex was a bit strange.) When the class sang the song again—after she died—he said, "I sat in the corner and sang real loud. I thought Lisa would come back, but she didn't." This made us both weep. This is why I put that particular song into the story. It just seemed right to do so.

When I wrote the book, it was really to try to make sense to myself of a tragedy that made no sense. I wasn't sure it was even a publishable story. So the response to Bridge to Terabithia *from so many people through the years of varying ages and nationalities has been astounding to me. I am especially*

awed by teachers like you who have brought the story into the classroom and used it to help children deal with the harder issues of life. I am very grateful.

With best wishes,
Katherine Paterson

What *is* all the fuss about reading aloud? **Some of you are already confused, aren't you?** Perhaps you didn't know there was a fuss. Well, there is—and there has been one for a very long time. Oh, it has ebbed and flowed as most things in education do, dependent upon the vagaries of the educational reform of the day; federal, state, or local politics; the new superintendent's policies; the lather fictitious parent Mrs. Hoochamadoochee has worked up; or the position on reading aloud taken by the one-and-only Gunilla Everspout, the literacy consultant who's been hired to "straighten out the teachers in this district."

Gunilla appeared recently in the school district of some very good friends of mine. A seismic blast that may have eclipsed the shot heard round the world was evidenced when she told some of my former graduate students that reading aloud could be likened to recess. (She would do well to steer clear of my automobile on rainy days when wet pavement is tolerated by the authorities as an excuse for out-of-control vehicles.) Needless to say, she did not view reading aloud to the students as any manner of instruction. As I listened to the stories of the conversation that ensued with her, I smiled knowingly, because I hear similar stories from all parts of the world on a regular basis.

There's the district reading coordinator with multiple degrees in literacy (including a postdoctorate) who told an eighth-grade teacher, "I'll come back someday when you're actually teaching" after discovering a read-aloud in process. Then, there's the kindergarten teacher who had a letter of reprimand put in her file by her principal for "wasting valuable instructional time reading aloud to the kindergartners." Or how about the third-grade teacher who asked for my help last year because his grade-level counterparts at the international school were preparing a "note of concern" for the administration because he was reading aloud to his students despite their request that he conform to their preference for no read-alouds above grade two? (Their classes were also three workbook pages ahead of his class, so you can see what a serious matter of educational import this was.) Did I mention the librarian who was told that reading to kids was not what she was paid to do—that she should be putting her master's degree in library science to work by *scanning books for checkout*? And, of course, we must not leave out my favorite parent, Mrs. Hoochamadoochee, who arrived unannounced for an appointment she never booked with me to share the news that she and several others at the P.T.O. were concerned about my reading aloud to children who were gifted, gifted, gifted, or the principal who told me that reading aloud is what lazy teachers do when they don't want to teach, or the colleague who told me I should "get on back to that elementary building" when I mentioned a great read-aloud for middle school kids. I could go on, but I don't need to, because many of you have your own stories. My point is—this book is aptly titled. The practice of reading aloud should not need a defense, but it does need one.

It's a bit discouraging to find that Gunilla Everspout and various members of the League of the Ill-Informed are everywhere—you can't escape running into them—yet it *is* rather heartening to discover that equally ubiquitous are teachers who care deeply about their instructional practice: teachers who desire to be well informed, knowledgeable, and articulate. Teachers like you. How do I know you care deeply about such things? It's easy. Teachers who don't are allergic to professional reading, and here you are with a professional book in your hands or on your electronic reader. Yay, you!

The Research Then

When I began work on my doctoral dissertation in the mid-1990s, it was clearly stressed by those who would determine my fate that my study needed to make a contribution to the profession. I knew, right from the start, that I would focus my research on the benefits of reading aloud to kids, and I was amazed to find a plethora of empirical research about the benefits. The studies I reviewed at that time noted gains in comprehension (Combs 1987; Elley and Mangubhai 1983; Labbo and Teale 1990; Morrow and Smith 1990; Richardson 1998; Yaden 1988; Yaden, Smolkin, and Conlon 1989); listening skills (Elley and Mangubhai 1983); enhancement of early reading skills (Durkin 1974; Huck 1979; Warren, Prater, and Griswold 1990); speaking skills (Chomsky 1972; Elley and Mangubhai 1983); vocabulary acquisition (Durkin 1981; Elley 1988, 1989; Hicks and Wadlington 1994; Maher 1991; Stahl, Richek, and Vandevier 1990); parental involvement (Cornell, Senechal, and Broda 1988; Robson and Whitley 1989; Warren, Prater, and Griswold 1990); and student motivation (Castle 1994; Herrold, Stanchfield, and Serabian 1989; Layne 1994; Trelease 1989; Wiesendanger and Bader 1989). I was, of course, also expected to note those studies that did *not* offer support for reading aloud as a form of "best practice."

I found none.

My research on incidental vocabulary acquisition by students from listening to teacher read-alouds (Layne 1996, 1998) was recognized with two awards; I mention that only to underscore the point that if I had purposely overlooked or even accidentally missed key studies that did not support the practice of reading aloud, it would have and should have been viewed as a major misstep in my review of the literature. Wouldn't someone on a research awards panel have caught such a glaring omission? Wouldn't one of my learned dissertation committee members have challenged it during my defense? Yet, not a word was spoken on that issue; I maintain it is because those who know the research are aware of the consistent findings in regard to the benefits of reading aloud to children and young adults. It is best practice. It is sound practice. Wan (2000) reviewed the literature of read-aloud as practice both in the home and at school and found, "There exists a strong body of research reporting the significance of reading aloud to children" (157). She went on to remark, "The report on what research has to say about the importance of read-aloud to children points to the significance of the topic" (158). Respected literacy researcher Patrick Shannon (2002) makes it clear, "The first rule of teaching literacy is to read to your kids" (6), and in the eyes of those educators who are professional enough to know why they do what they do, it is blasphemy to speak a word against such a necessary and beneficial practice.

There is a key point I want to make about the research on teachers reading aloud to their students that I believe deserves a solid shout-out, and it is this one. More research needs to be conducted with older students. Many great educators jump to the assumption that reading aloud is what we do "for the little ones," and when that is the mind-set of some practitioners, it is easy for the researchers to follow suit. Nancie Atwell is quite transparent in her 1998 book *In the Middle* when she says, "For a long time I thought of reading aloud as something teachers in the elementary grades did to entertain young children" (144). I found Nancie's confession heartening at the time, and I still do. If an educator of her distinguished caliber can, at one time, have held that assumption, it should come as no surprise that others—be they teachers, parents, or community members—may hold it as well.

The Research Now

There has been a discernible uptick in authors and researchers calling attention to the issue of teachers reading aloud to older students (Allen 2000; Albright and Ariail 2005; Ariail and Albright 2006; Beers and Samuels 1996; Ficklen and Brooks 2011; Fisher and Frey 2008; Gidlund 2011; Ivey 2003; Ivey and Broaddus 2001; Layne 2009; Lesesne

2006; Press, Henenberg, and Getman 2009; Prus 2008; Rycik and Irvin 2005; Trelease 2013; Wilson 1999; Zehr 2010), but I'd still like to see more because I believe the practice of reading aloud is called into question with older students more frequently than with younger ones and because reading aloud reportedly decreases as grade level increases (Delo 2008; Duchein and Mealey 1993; Hoffman, Roser, and Battle 1993; Richardson 2000; Trelease 2013). I struggled mightily at the time of my study to find work being done on the benefits of reading aloud to older students. The issue had received a bit of attention (Anders and Levine 1990; Davidson and Koppenhaver 1993; Jennings 1990; Maher 1991; Richardson 1981, 1994; Stahl, Richek, and Vandevier 1990), but the quantity was scant when compared with the work done with younger children (Clay 1979; Cochran-Smith 1984; Durkin 1974, 1979; Elley 1988, 1989; Feitelson, Kita, and Goldstein 1986; Lomax 1976; Morrow 1983; Ninio 1980; Ninio and Bruner 1978; Robbins and Ehri 1994; Roser and Martinez 1985; Schickedanz 1978, 1981; Taylor 1983; Warren, Prater, and Griswold 1990; Yaden 1988; Yaden, Smolkin, and Conlon 1989). I was, however, heartened by Routman's strong voice in *Invitations* (1991) when she boldly stated, "Reading aloud should take place daily at all grade levels, including junior high and high school" (32). Although I didn't know Regie at the time, her words gave me added courage—the confidence to know that I wasn't crazy after all, no matter what they were saying down in the teachers' lounge!

I focused my dissertation research on students in fourth grade in large part out of necessity and proximity because I was still a full-time classroom teacher, and most of my solid contacts were at the elementary level in those days. My true desire would have been to conduct the study with students in grade seven, but we work with what we have at many points along life's path. I had access to fourth graders, and they were still a giant step beyond the age groups used in most quantitative studies I had found in the area of read-alouds. I keep my eye on the fine research being done on read-alouds today yet still feel the need to send out the request for more work on the effect of reading aloud with upper-grade students.

Another point I'll make with regard to the research I have read in recent years is that there remains a consistent yet often disregarded fuel to the read-aloud fire. We continue to see empirical results and hear respected voices telling us "this is good for kids" and "here is why it is good for kids" at all grade levels. Listening to teacher read-alouds benefits students' syntactic development (Lane and Wright 2007; Mokhtari and

Thompson 2006); vocabulary acquisition (Beck and McKeown 2001; Kindle 2009; McGee and Schickedanz 2007; Routman 2003; Santoro, Chard, Howard, and Baker 2008; Sinatra 2008); comprehension (Elster 1994; Knoth 1998; Kraemer, McCabe, and Sinatra 2012; Richardson 2000; Santoro, Chard, Howard, and Baker 2008; Sipe 2000; Smolkin and Donovan 2001; Teale 2003); fluency (Hurst, Scales, Frecks, and Lewis 2011; Tompkins 2006; Trelease 2013); and reading skills such as pronunciation and inflection (Albright and Ariail 2005; Carbo 1996; Routman 2003). Read-alouds improve our students' writing (Polette 2005); their engagement (Albright and Ariail 2005; Morrison and Wlodarczyk 2009); their attitudes (Braun 2010; Krashen 2004; Layne 2009; Trelease 2013); and their understanding of text types (Donovan, Milewicz, and Smolkin 2003). Hearing text read aloud also broadens students' thinking as well as their imaginations (Coiro 2000) and affords them the opportunity to become more culturally sensitive (Irvine and Armento 2001; Morgan 2009; Routman 2003; Verden 2012). Finally, the intimacy of the read-aloud experience builds rapport between a teacher and his or her students (Atwell 2007; Pardeck 1990; Routman 2003), providing for a bibliotherapeutic environment that promotes a deepening emotional intelligence (Bauer and Balius 1995; Forgan and Gonzalez-DeHass 2004; Jackson and Panyan 2002; Sullivan and Strang 2002). Yet despite overwhelming evidence for the dramatic effect of reading aloud *throughout the grades,* every new policy, trend, or initiative attempting to reshape education "based on research" appears to be led by a team of individuals ignorant of a body of evidence that perhaps laid its most serious claim to fame in the mid-1980s with the Report of the Commission on Reading's landmark study *Becoming a Nation of Readers* (Anderson, Hiebert, Scott, and Wilkinson 1985). Those of you who are read-aloud enthusiasts and who are old enough to have followed the research evolution in this area were expecting to read these oft-cited words from that seminal report, "The single most important activity for building the knowledge required for eventual success in reading is reading aloud to children" (23). Equally important, in my mind, is the contention of these researchers that "reading aloud should be emphasized not only in the home but also in the classroom, continuously throughout grades K–12" (51). The commission's findings received additional support in 1998 when the National Research Council (Snow, Burns, and Griffin) recommended the use of read-alouds. Why don't we jump all the way back to 1924 to the very first volume of *The Horn Book* when Anne Eaton was espousing the reasons for reading aloud or fast-forward from there to 2012, when an illuminating study involving the importance of read-alouds reported by Worthy, Chamberlain, Peterson, Sharp, and Shih was published in *Literacy Research and Instruction?* If we all want to be "research based" (and it seems to me that these days nearly everyone does), then why don't we listen to such a significant and consistent body of evidence? Why does it appear to be the case that "public education has marginalized such practices" (Worthy et al. 2012, 308)?

In an article from 2005, Giorgis, Johnson, Forsburg, and DeJong open with this statement: "In an age of No Child Left Behind, high-stakes testing, and curriculum overload, time for reading aloud is often viewed as expendable" (89). Thank goodness we have evolved ten years forward in 2015 to find the practice of reading aloud finally receiving the attention it merits—based on research, right (insert sarcastic laugh)? Oh, don't tell me you missed its pronounced emphasis in all the literature as an instructional practice for helping our students achieve the Common Core State Standards. How about in the new district curriculum guide—you saw it focused on there, maybe? Well, surely it's been the subject of serious discussion around the table at those cross-grade-level language arts committee meetings—what with everyone wanting to be research based and all. Or . . . more likely, the best and brightest are pulling the shades and closing the doors (posting guards on a rotation schedule in grades six and above) for fear of being "caught" frittering away valuable instructional time reading aloud to their students. And those in the know are left with the question I've been asking for more than two decades: Why doesn't our practice match our verbalized intent?

Leading in Literacy

I hear leaders in schools around the world profess what I believe to be an earnest desire for the practice in their teachers' classrooms to be based on research, and yet I regularly hear stories from teachers who have been or are being terrorized by administrators, colleagues, parents, or out-of-control school board members who don't know their place (don't get me started) because students are being read to during the school day. The good news is that I finally received a satisfactory answer to my question Why doesn't our practice match our verbalized intent?

It came during a memorable dinner (we call it the heart-and-mind dinner) with my dear friend Regie Routman. We were despairing of our unsuccessful efforts to change the world of education and vowing to keep fighting the fight when I suddenly felt inclined to ask her my question. Though read-alouds had not been the topic of our conversation before that moment, I had been working on this book, and it suddenly came to my mind right in the middle of our dinner. So I asked her, "Regie, why doesn't classroom practice with regard to reading aloud match the intent we hear from people who claim a desire to follow research-based best practice?" And in her sage way she said quite simply, "Steven, teachers must be leaders—and leaders must know literacy." Well, there you have it, and best of all, it rings with truth.

How many people do you know in a key leadership role in a school building or district who truly know literacy best practices and—stay with me here—have the *authority* to put them in place? I know very few in school leadership who possess both the depth and breadth of knowledge I'm talking about, and this means that those individuals must rely on someone, somewhere to help them lead in literacy. And the selection of that individual or team of individuals by a well-meaning administrator can lead to all manner of disastrous consequences if they do not choose wisely. Gunilla Everspout and her winged monkeys can do a lot of damage fast; I have picked up the pieces enough times to know.

And so I must echo Regie's statement: we need teachers to become leaders—leaders who know literacy! Does that mean you all have to become the principal or the superintendent of schools? No (though it would certainly help if some of you did). You can lead from the classroom—if you know your stuff! Reflective practitioners not only ponder why what's working is working or why it's not, but know why they are doing what they are doing in the first place. The kind of leaders I am talking about have a rationale that they can articulate with confidence to anyone who asks. If someone asks you why you're reading aloud to the third graders and your first response is "Because it's *so* much fun, and we all enjoy it," we're in trouble. Big trouble. We're not in trouble because you're wrong. No, it's fine to include that as the seventeenth bullet point of your calculated and confidence-inspiring response. We're in trouble because that's too fluffy an answer to be your first go-to when someone is questioning your pedagogy. You sound like a Smurf. Stop it. You're an educator—you need to sound like one.

This is where the decision to advance your own professional development is critical, in my opinion. And I don't mean for one year, I mean for the rest of your life. If you're going to lead, you've got to grow—so get into the most rigorous master's in literacy program around. If it's too easy to get in, look somewhere else. Already have a master's degree but it's not in literacy? Get another one. Finished with that? Time for the doctorate! In between, head to a new professional conference on literacy every year. Read one professional book on literacy for every guilty-pleasure book you pick up. Share your knowledge with your faculty, your district, the state, the country, and the world by speaking at conferences or doing some writing. This is how professionals behave, and it is how they learn to lead.

Anyone who knows me well would tell you that I do not mind someone asking me a question, but I hate being questioned. There is a world of difference between the two. The primary reason I kept pushing forward in my education was that I wanted to be more informed than I was about my practice—and I wanted people to know that I was well informed. I watched a huge change occur in the way everyone interacted with me as I became more knowledgeable. I was rarely questioned, but I was often sought out by those who had questions. I will tell you that my desire to become a more knowledgeable practitioner came about, in large part, because I was tired—tired of having to defend the practice of reading aloud to my students. I had read to them in every grade I had ever taught from primary through grade eight, and I was questioned about that practice all along the way.

Mrs. Hoochamadoochee, the fictitious parent I have named to represent every nightmare parent I've met in my career, came to see me when I was teaching fifth grade. Her opening line was, just as it is when she comes to see *you*, "Well, I'm not usually one to say anything . . ." There is a special cell in Parent Jail for all who begin their conversations with teachers using those words, but I typically have kept quiet about it.

She went on to explain that she and a few mothers had been talking about me "down at the PTO." I hid my grimace and reached nonchalantly for my grade book so as to keep my hands occupied with something outside the scope of her throat. I was tempted to say, "I understand. I've been talking about you with several colleagues down in the teachers' lounge," but I held my tongue lest I meet with the unemployment line. She continued, "Well, Dr. Layne, the mothers and I were talking about my Harriet. She's gifted, you know." (Aren't they always?) I nodded, fearful of speaking. "Anyway," she forged ahead, "Harriet reports that you've been reading aloud to fifth graders, and um, I'm just not sure how to put this delicately, Dr. Layne . . ."

"Oh, I'm sure you'll find a way." (Did I say that? Oh, dear. I did.) Crevices were forming in the floodgates of my steely determination to keep my mouth shut. Mother has always said my resolve to behave well quickly dissolves when I am forced to interact with crazy people for even short bouts of time. Fortunately, Mrs. H. was too caught up in trying to construct coherent thoughts to notice my comment.

"Well, the mothers and I were thinking that maybe instead of reading to the fifth graders you could sort of, you know, um, *teach*. After all, that *is* what we pay you to do, isn't it? And when you think about it, we *are* the taxpayers, so we *do* pay your salary."

WARNING: This professional book is about to turn into a crime novel—a murder mystery, without the mystery part. This will be one of those where you know who the killer is right from the start, and you empathize with him and write him letters in prison saying you would have done the same thing.

No, no, no. I didn't really commit a heinous act of violence against Mrs. H. I couldn't because I had faced situations like this when I taught second and third grades— and would go on to face them in sixth through eighth grades. In that moment Mrs. H. blurred in my vision and became a colleague who mocked me, an administrator who reprimanded me, a consultant who condescended to me, and—of course—a host of other parents who questioned me. So, I didn't hurt her because I was used to it by then.

People don't understand.

They don't understand because they are not knowledgeable; the danger lies in the solitary fact that they are unaware of how little they know. Sadly, education is different from every other career. I have a brain, yet the idea that I would try to coach my brain surgeon (if I needed one—which I do *not*. Yet.) in surgery is ridiculous. I have also been in many hospitals, but I would not endeavor to tell the CEO how to run the hospital. Why? Because I am smart enough to have a healthy awareness of how much I don't know.

Most everyone has been to school, and in the views of the general public, there is very little about school of which they do not feel they have a thorough understanding. They've all been taught, so they know all about teaching—they think. And it's not just the parents and community members. Such attitudes come, sometimes, from administrators who haven't taught nearly long enough in a variety of classroom settings, from teachers whose professional growth plan involves teaching a decent forty-one-minute lesson once a year so they can skate through their evaluations, and consultants who consult on *any* need your school has—it just so happens that whatever your area of need is, that's their specialty!

I want to bring us full circle now by pointing out that a fuss over reading aloud can come about very quickly—without much warning at all, really. And ideally, I've been able to start you thinking about why it can come and from whom it might come. Most important, though, I want to challenge you to be ready for the fuss, and to manage it politely and professionally before it turns into a battle. There are a lot more citations in this chapter than you would typically find in this kind of a book, I know, but they are provided to help you strengthen your position. I encourage you to seek out the full articles and read them thoughtfully and carefully so that you can be articulate in defending a practice that years of research have told us is both necessary and beneficial. I bet you know the other reason I want you to find and read some of those articles, don't you? Because it is what professionals do. It's also what leaders do, and I want my readers to *become* leaders. Leaders—in literacy. So please, spread the word.

∾ Position Statement

There Is No Doubt: My Position on Teacher Read-Alouds in the Classroom

Jerry L. Johns

Northern Illinois University—Illinois, USA
Distinguished Teaching Professor Emeritus
International Literacy Association President
2002–2003

As a classroom teacher in the elementary school, I prioritized the daily schedule so there would be time to share a read-aloud with my students. The read-aloud was a regular part of the school day, typically when students returned from the lunch period and recess. Students knew the routine; they entered the classroom and took their seats in anticipation of the read-aloud time. It was a relaxing time for us. Sometimes there was brief sharing before or after the reading, but most of the time students just listened as I read to them. Some watched me read, and others rested their heads on their desks.

There were even times when some students had their copy of the book I was reading and followed along. I knew they were really following along when they highlighted the miscues I had made while reading. Sometimes I used this information in a later lesson to discuss significant and nonsignificant miscues.

I'd like to think that I read aloud to my students every day, but that would not be true. There were assemblies and other changes in the schedule that eliminated the read-aloud during our regularly scheduled time. If, however, the book was particularly interesting to students, they would ask me to read later in the day. I took that as a positive sign.

Other teachers in the school also read to their students. One teacher (Cal) read Old Yeller *to his classes year after year. Students came to expect to hear that book read aloud in his class because word got around. And when Cal came into the teachers' lounge in a particularly somber and quiet mood, I remember asking, "You're at the part in the book again, right?"*

When I joined the Faculty in Reading at Northern Illinois University, I continued to promote read-alouds to my undergraduate and graduate students as an important part of a balanced reading program. I stressed daily read-alouds, but also told my students that they could miss a few days each school year and not feel guilty. I also encouraged them to share a wide range of books. Not every book would be a winner with students, and some books that worked well one year would not have the same effect the following year. The main point was to read aloud to students.

A research study in The Reading Teacher *revealed that the number of teachers reading aloud to their students decreased through the grades. In addition, not that many teachers were reading daily to their students. I renewed my efforts to promote daily read-alouds in my university reading courses and when I was invited to schools for staff development and in-service sessions. There were even a few instances when I worked with staff members to develop read-aloud lists for each grade level in their school. I also shared my list of ten reasons why teachers should read aloud to students:*

1. Stimulates language development

2. Helps students move naturally into reading

3. Shows that reading is pleasurable

4. Demonstrates that print is meaningful

5. Fosters an interest in books

6. Stimulates students to react to what is read

7. Helps create favorable attitudes toward reading

8. Encourages students to listen actively

9. Serves as a model

10. Builds rapport

You can probably add some of your own reasons to the list. Steven Layne, the author of this book, would undoubtedly add "helps build vocabulary" as a result of his dissertation research. The benefits of reading aloud to students are many, but there linger significant challenges.

A 2014 article by Clark and Andreasen in volume 53 of Literacy Research and Instruction *(162–182) explores student perceptions of teacher read-alouds. It arrived in the mail shortly after I received Steve's invitation to share my thoughts on read-alouds. Clearly, challenges remain if we are to fully embrace read-alouds as an essential part of classroom instruction in reading. It would be great to see read-alouds become a staple in our instructional programs regardless of what happens to be in vogue at a particular time in the history of reading instruction. You can make read-alouds an ongoing reality—at least in your classroom. Just make the commitment.*

∾ Position Statement

Are Teacher Read-Alouds the Swiss Army Knife of Effective Reading and Writing Pedagogy?

Brian Cambourne

University of Wollongong—New South Wales,
  Australia
Principal Fellow
International Literacy Association, William S. Gray
  Citation of Merit 2012

Teachers have always read aloud to their students. In fact it's probably one of the most widely used classroom practices found in our schools. I know this because I recently posed this question to Mr. Google: "Why should teachers read aloud to their students?" In the space of 0.36 seconds, he identified 104,000,000 (that's 104 million!) references, articles, citations, reports, and other texts that addressed my question. Although I didn't read every one of those 104 million entries, my impression from sampling the first twenty or so pages was that the overwhelming majority of the references were very positive about the value and power of teachers reading aloud to their students.

Sprinkled among the 104 million references was a plethora of research claims about the efficacy of regular sessions of teachers reading aloud in class. Among other things this research showed that teacher read-alouds could be used to "demonstrate the power of stories," "provide insights into how reading works," "show how to search for meaning," "demonstrate how to make connections and inferences," "develop new vocabulary and syntactic awareness," "stimulate imagination," "expose students to a range of litera-ture," "help distinguish different genres," "encourage a lifelong enjoyment of reading," "help learner-writers identify and transfer the literary devices authors use to their own writing," and much, much more.

IN DEFENSE *of* READ-ALOUD

What's this got to do with the Swiss Army Knife (SAK)? I think the SAK is a useful metaphor for challenging our traditional perceptions of the teacher read-aloud and opening it up to new possibilities. When I visualize the SAK, I see a compact container of handy tools such as a screwdriver, nail file, corkscrew, toothpick, scissors, and tweezers. Furthermore this picture invokes a range of associated meanings such as these: an SAK is portable and convenient; it can be carried with you anywhere; and you can reach for it anytime, open it up, and quickly select the tool you need for filing your nails, opening wine, tightening a loose screw, and so on. With some of the newer versions you can add new tools—some SAKs have more than eighty attachments!

Think about it. Like the SAK, a teacher read-aloud time is an extremely portable entity that all teachers can carry with them from class to class. Like the SAK, a teacher read-aloud event is a multipurpose, versatile, one-stop pedagogical tool (or platform) for creating a multiplicity of mindful, contextualized opportunities for learners to engage with the multiplicity of skills and knowledge that effective readers and writers need to control.

Finally, like the SAK, the teacher read-aloud has its own set of "basic" tools that can be opened and applied. These are the conditions of learning that I believe underpin effective human learning. Regular teacher read-alouds are a form of immersion that creates opportunities for a multitude of demonstrations about learning, language, and all the other accoutrements of effective reading, writing, spelling, grammar, text structure, and so on. Furthermore, teacher read-alouds are inherently engaging, providing opportunities to communicate expectations and to respond to learners' approximations—leading to opportunities for learners to employ their burgeoning skills and knowledge about reading and writing, and to take responsibility for applying such skills and knowledge to the real world.

Chapter 2

Establishing a Successful
Read-Aloud Time

Dear Ms. Lowry,

My name is Suz St. John, and I am a kindergarten teacher. I'd like to tell you the absolutely true story of "How Mrs. St. John's Kindergartners Came to Love and Admire *Gooney Bird Greene*."

This past summer I was searching for a chapter book to read to my students. I wanted to challenge my students with a read-aloud that had a complex storyline and vivid characters yet limited illustrations. I knew I needed a book with tangible characters in order for my kindergartners to bond with them. A friend recommended your book *Gooney Bird Greene*. With my first reading, I knew that this was *the* read-aloud to begin the school year with; this book would inspire my fledgling storytellers. I could not wait to share *Gooney Bird Greene*!

And so, in September, we began. I must admit, it was a rocky start. For my visually dependent, young students the concept of listening to a book without illustrations on every page was difficult to grasp. But we persevered, and as we did, your vibrant descriptions made Gooney Bird come alive. My students learned to visualize as we read of Gooney Bird's red hair, eclectic fashions, and spirited personality. As Gooney Bird's character developed, our admiration grew.

My students admired Gooney Bird's creative storytelling and her bold, unique fashion sense. (Free wardrobe rein is sheer delight to a five-year-old!) I admire the role model Gooney Bird is for all students, but especially for young girls. She's intelligent, independent, and vivacious—with a strong sense of self. What teacher would not wish this for all her female students? From our admiration came my class's first questions: Is Gooney Bird Greene based on a real person? Is she someone you know? Is she "you" as a little girl or a combination of people?

As we continued to read, we pictured ourselves in Mrs. Pidgeon's classroom, sitting at a desk, listening to Gooney Bird's absolutely true stories. We giggled every time Gooney Bird's fanciful stories turned out to be extraordinarily normal. And as we listened, more questions arose. Where did the ideas for Gooney Bird's stories come from? Are these true events or your vision of the wishful adventures of a young, spirited girl?

My students were sad when the book came to an end. They wanted more Gooney Bird stories. I assured them that we would someday hear more (yeah, sequels!), but that right now, they had a job to do. I explained that inside each one of them is a storyteller just like Gooney Bird and that I could not wait to hear all the extraordinary normal things that happen to them each and every day. Their faces were beaming.

And that, Ms. Lowry, is the absolutely true story of how my class grew to love and admire Gooney Bird Greene. We anxiously await your response! (Because being patient is hard when you are five.)

In admiration and gratitude,
Suz St. John

Kindergarten
Howard B. Thomas Grade School
Burlington, Illinois

Dear Mrs. St. John,

What a treat to hear about your students and their new friendship with Gooney Bird Greene. It has been great fun for me to write about her (I've most recently finished the sixth book in the series!). I never went to second grade myself. And that's actually part of the reason I created these books.

When I finished first grade, I was told that I would go to third grade the next year. All of my good friends from school were in the second-grade classroom, with a cheerful teacher named Mrs. Tay. But each morning I walked past its door—and could hear their voices and laughter inside—and trudged upstairs to the third-grade room where I didn't know anyone, and where I had a very grouchy teacher. I yearned to be in second grade, and that feeling never left me—that I somehow missed out on a wonderful year.

I yearned for something else as well, and that was to be popular and self-confident, instead of the shy and uninteresting person I really was.

So, years later, I created Gooney Bird, the little girl I wished I could have been, and put her in the classroom I had never had. When, in the first book, she says, "I want a desk right smack in the middle of everything!" I could picture my own seven-year-old self, who wanted the same thing but was much too timid to ask for it.

I'm glad your kindergarten students have enjoyed the stories about Gooney Bird—and by Gooney Bird—and I hope they have all found their own wonderful stories to tell.

With love,
Lois Lowry

Just because you do something doesn't mean you're any good at it. We've all met people who are not self-aware enough to see the truth or whose egos won't allow them to admit the truth, which is that they have a tendency to devote a fair amount of time to something they are not particularly skilled at doing—and it isn't getting any better. It causes the rest of us great consternation when it turns out that the aforementioned description applies to such individuals' professions rather than their hobbies, but we won't linger on that one lest some of you begin shouting names aloud before realizing you are in an environment in which this could lead to unemployment. The point I want to make is that if reading aloud is instruction (and it is), then we need to consider how to make a read-aloud time successful. Remember, just because we do it doesn't mean it's good. And we aren't even going for good here—we're all about great! So, in this chapter I want to share with you some suggestions for crafting a truly outstanding read-aloud time.

Seating Plan

One key consideration in creating a successful read-aloud time is the seating plan. Some of you are jumping to the conclusion that I mean a diagram showing exactly where everyone will be. Relax. That is not at all what I mean by seating plan. Think about this, though. Who among us prepares to enjoy text by looking for the most uncomfortable place in the house to sit? In general, people looking to enjoy text want to be comfortable, and a cold, hard desk is not the best choice. When I'm reading aloud, I want kids to forget their surroundings and truly enter the story in every sense; this is more easily accomplished when they are comfortable. That being said, sometimes we have no choice. The room may not allow the space to get kids out of desks, there may not be a reading lounge to take them to, or you may decide that the amount of time you will be reading on a given day doesn't warrant the move.

That's all okay, but it must not prevent us from understanding what is, undoubtedly, the best-case scenario. I think, too, that we are obligated to try to do what we can to resolve this issue favorably. If read-aloud is instruction, then the environment merits consideration. When teaching basketball skills, don't we often demand a gymnasium or an outdoor court? When working with calculus, don't we request calculators?

When I began working in a junior high school classroom and lost my more spacious elementary classroom, I was in a bit of a snit. Where did these kids get their giant bodies? Between their huge bodies that were invariably sprawling from Chicago to Sacramento and the mammoth desks that contained those bodies, I was lucky I had room to stand and teach, yet I couldn't bear the thought of my students being housed in desks during my read-aloud time. It took me a week to figure it out, but I did solve the dilemma. I created a map of where every desk had to be moved so that we gained a big open area. Next, I assigned students (every period of the day) to know the new temporary location of their desks, and we practiced. They were like trained seals within a week! They could "open" the room up with a nice big space for read-aloud time or put it back for instruction in less than a minute. As we all became more experienced at it, that minute of "room reorganization" often began just as the period dismissal bell was about to ring so that the room was already set for the next class when they arrived (with a few seconds stolen from the passing period).

Though I didn't realize it at first, upon reflection I came to understand that the thought I put into solving this dilemma actually underscored to my students how serious I was about the time I spent reading aloud. Why? Because read-aloud time is instruction, and I needed to work earnestly at providing the best environment for my students to "plug in" to the text I was intending to share. I remember Ronnie Kadra saying to me one day, "Dr. Layne, you turn the whole classroom upside down just to read to us." I responded, "Yes, I do, Ronnie. You're just that important."

Environment can be easier at the elementary level because *sometimes* the elementary teachers have larger rooms, and the students generally have smaller bodies. Some of you are yelling, I know. There's a third-grade teacher from Florida screaming, "Have you seen the closet they put me in!" Let's remember I am talking in generalities. I had a fairly normal-sized classroom when I began teaching elementary school, but with smaller bodies and smaller desks, I was able to carve out a niche that I called Mr. Layne's Reading Corner. I made the sign myself and hung it proudly in a corner of the classroom. Because of a prudent fiscal plan I had instituted, I was able to purchase a blue beanbag chair and a large purple pillow from Target during the week just before school started and place them in what I then considered my classroom Reading Utopia. Keep in mind this was early in my career so I had not yet amassed the wealth that I was certain a teacher's salary would later bring and that would subsequently provide funding for at least two beanbags and three pillows.

When the children arrived on that very first day of my career, I began by giving them a tour of our classroom just as my methods instructor had taught me to do. I was nearly bursting with pride as we approached Mr. Layne's Reading Corner. William didn't notice the sign, but I was quick to point it out. I must confess that I was waiting all day for the moment when I would call them over to this area, and in my young teacher naïveté was completely unprepared for the devastation to come.

Once everyone was nicely settled back from lunch, I called them from their desks to come to Mr. Layne's Reading Corner and was nearly toppled by the mass exodus of children from their desks. There was shouting and screaming and clutching and grabbing. I feared for my life! Feathers were flying from my pillow, and beans were departing the beanbag chair at an alarming rate. I remember thinking, *They didn't teach us about this in our methods classes!* And then I entered the fray and shouted, "Children, stop this insanity THIS INSTANT!" They became quiet because I was brimming with ferocity. I explained then, "I have a system, you see. A system for managing the seating in Mr. Layne's Reading Corner."

At the moment I spoke the words, I hadn't the slightest idea what my system was, but then I spied some note cards on a shelf. I walked toward them with the air of a person who was quite in charge. I ceremoniously uncapped a blue marker and then a purple one. I drew a blue circle on one note card and a purple square on the other one. "Now, children, these are *passes!*" I reached into my hat of names and drew out two. "Melissa will have the blue beanbag, and Robert will have the purple pillow for the next week and that, you see, is that." I tacked my new system to the bulletin board for all to see. "Now," I continued, "there is no need to maim the innocent in a rush to Mr. Layne's Reading Corner because we already know who is getting the favored seats this week. Any questions?"

A tiny sprite smiled at me. Her name was Heather. I can still see her face as she said, "Teacher, may we share?" Ohhhh, my teacher heart sang for joy. I swear I heard angels singing in the heavenly choir at that moment. This is why I had become a teacher.

I pulled a chair over and sat down next to Heather. "Why, Heather, yes! *Yes*, you may share. My classroom is going to be all about sharing. You see, children, this is our *learning community*, and I want sharing to play a major role in everything we do here."

By the end of the third day, I was *so done* with sharing. These crazy children were at me every second! "Melissa said she was going to share the beanbag with me, but then she shared it with Tiffany, and now I hate her!" And "Robert said we could *both* share his pillow with him, but there isn't room for all three of us, and he's crying, Mr. Layne, because he let us have it, but we didn't tell him to, he just did." And "Melissa won't share the beanbag unless you get her milk for her. She said that yesterday at lunch, and I got her milk, but then she let Kelly . . ."

"NO SHARING!" I erupted like a dormant volcano come to life. "I don't want to hear the word *share* from anyone for the rest of the day. Got it? Melissa will use her beanbag, and Robert will use his pillow, and no one else will so much as allow the hem of their garment to brush against the beanbag or the pillow for the remainder of the week. And if Melissa is absent, NO ONE WILL USE THE BEANBAG! DON'T EVEN ASK!"

So, let's just say that despite my advocacy for "getting them out of desks," you may want to have a plan that is a bit more well developed than my original one. Once I had a handle on my seating "pass" system, it actually worked quite well, and over the years I amassed a wide range of special "seats" that made the reading area all the more enjoyable for my elementary students. This gave way, of course, to the reading lounges that I advocate so strongly for in my book *Igniting a Passion for Reading* (Layne 2009). If you work in a middle or high school, or if your elementary classroom can barely house Stuart Little and his family, get moving on the reading lounge as a top priority!

I will say again, the time spent reading aloud has to make the seating issue relevant enough for you to take action. If you are an eighth-grade social studies teacher, for example, and you plan to use your read-aloud simply to start class for five minutes each day, desks will work fine. But to that same social studies teacher, I would say that a lot of kids will have trouble following the read-aloud for only five minutes a day until after you've "hooked them." So, maybe you do make some open space or use the library or reading lounge during the launch of the book. You can't really launch well on five minutes a day, but if you spend a full period or a period and a half drawing kids into the story, you will be able to move to five minutes a day. More on launching in a moment.

Once everyone has a seat, you're finally ready to get to work. And it *is* work. I believe many people really believe that's not the case. I've run across my fair share of well-educated individuals who believe that read-aloud time involves nothing more than the teacher grabbing up some text and beginning to orally read. That's a far cry from what's happening when I'm at the helm, and I'm sure the same is true for many of my readers. Taking sixth graders into the future for Rodman Philbrick's *The Last Book in the Universe* (2000) and making them believe they are really there, transporting first graders back in time for

Sally Walker's *The 18 Penny Goose* (1998) and allowing them to worry over Solomon the goose's fate, or carting tenth graders into the turbulent home of empathic Brewster Rawlins in Neal Shusterman's *Bruiser* (2010) and forcing them to consider how similar their own actions might be to those of the main character is major work if you know what you are doing. It's very hard work. In fact, it is such hard work that I hate, loathe, and despise interruptions when I'm in the midst of it.

Do Not Disturb

I put a Do Not Disturb sign on my door when I was reading aloud for most of my career. It's true. My colleague Kathy Bruni has on many occasions regaled me with the story of the terrified seventh grader she sent to ask me if we could head to our favorite deli for lunch one day. Apparently, he returned ashen because my sign was out. He had been my student before he had been hers, so he knew full well my feeling about being interrupted when I am reading aloud. As the story goes, he told her, "Mrs. Bruni, if you want to know if he's free for lunch, then you're going to have to go down there and ask him yourself. I'm not knocking on his door when he's got that sign out. It's a death wish!"

Although the story is good for a chuckle, think about what was being communicated to my students (and colleagues) about how important I considered read-aloud time. I have many a school secretary who can testify that the school day went more smoothly if they avoided a device I referred to as "the squawk box" during my read-aloud time. I would on most occasions give them note cards listing my read-aloud time for the day or week and ask them to avoid interrupting my room during those times with some emergency such as "Julia forgot to circle her salad dressing choice on her hot food day order form. Could she please come to the office, Dr. Layne?" Might I be so bold as to suggest in such cases that Julia make do with whatever salad dressing is available and thus learn to circle her choices in the future? It's thinking like that, my wife assures me, that kept people from suggesting I ever become the principal of a school.

Of course, most teachers don't care for the "squawk box" much, and few of us care to ever be interrupted when we are teaching. For me, though, and perhaps for some of you, my decision to use the Do Not Disturb sign made it clear to my students that something they might presume to be less important than "real instruction" was actually just as important as everything else we did. My elevation of it, in actuality, ended up making it equal with the other types of instruction in which I engaged.

Again back to the reading lounges from my earlier book—once a room like that is in place, there is no need for the Do Not Disturb sign anymore, because when a class is in the lounge, nobody interrupts. Why? The whole building gets the message. People know you're busy before they even look in the window!

Launching a Read-Aloud

Effective instruction involves planning; that's as sound of a pedagogical statement as you're likely to read anywhere. When it comes to read-aloud time, a key component of effectiveness involves what I call the "launch" of a new book you intend to read aloud to your students.

The launch, in my mind, refers to the actual beginning of the read-aloud. Anything up to that point that a teacher may have done to build interest in an upcoming read-aloud title (book trailers, reviews posted in the classroom, visit to the author's website, and that all-important thorough preview of the book) would be considered "prelaunch" in my mind. Think of it in terms of a rocket if you like. When the rocket is "launching," it's hitting the air. When you are *launching* your read-aloud, you're starting to actually read it.

To avoid any confusion, I need to specify here that when I talk about the launch of a title, I am always talking about lengthier works—not picture books. Of course we can and should read picture books aloud, but they do not necessitate the kind of launching I am discussing in this section. For those who have ever successfully read a lengthier piece of text (one that takes several days, weeks, or months) to kids, you all know when you have reached the point where you can say with assurance, "I've got them! They are totally hooked—can't wait to hear more!" Right? Do you know what I am describing? If you don't know, imagine it. You're barely in the door from the hallway, and you are practically accosted by students panting, drooling, and begging, "Are you going to read some more of that book today? You *are*, aren't you?"

Everything you've done to reach the point where you know you have captivated the group is either part of your prelaunch or part of your actual launch. Once you "have them under your spell," the book has been successfully launched! A successful book launch requires you to select the right title for the right time, of course, but we'll talk more about that in Chapter 3. For now, let's assume you have selected the right title at the right time. What other components need to be considered in launching successfully?

In my experience, genre is a tremendous consideration. Launching a multicultural title, or a high fantasy, science fiction, or historical fiction chapter book or novel requires far more complex concentration from your listeners and much more careful and intentional scaffolding from you than a realistic fiction story. Likewise, a nonfiction piece, depending on the topic, could require significant activation of schema and much deeper thinking than a realistic story set in a familiar location. It is critical that teachers understand this and that we take action to address it.

When teachers tell me stories of "read-alouds gone bad" and ask for a diagnosis, one of the first areas I discuss with them is the launch of the book. For example, let's say that a sixth-grade language arts teacher faithfully reads aloud to her class three days a week for ten to fifteen minutes each day. (She can do that because she has a double period of language arts, uninterrupted for eighty to ninety minutes a day, just as God intended it to be. *Don't* get me started on that topic, or I'll never finish the book.) Well, that *might* work if she's reading *Blood on His Hands* (Roberts 2004), but it's likely to be a problem if she's reading *The Giver* (Lowry 1993). Why? Because *Blood on His Hands* is a realistic fiction story, which means that our students' prior knowledge has significant merit, and *The Giver* is a dystopian sci-fi novel set in a futuristic community, which limits the value of our students' prior knowledge significantly.

No matter the grade level, when we are asking kids to enter a genre that will demand more from them in terms of careful thought and when they are "listening up" in terms of the sophistication of the story, outstanding instruction will be required if we are, in fact, going to captivate the entire group rather than just a few bright stars. I learned over several years that if I wanted to read aloud *The Giver* in grade seven, it would necessitate a tremendous amount of start-and-stop during the launch phase. For example, the opening line of the book says, "It was almost December, and Jonas was beginning to be frightened" (1). Okay, we've reached my first stopping point in the read-aloud. I've read only a sentence, and I'm already stopping for discussion. Why? Because I am the master of the text in terms of bringing it successfully to the students. I know where we are headed—into a setting that is *very* different from where my students live. Those readers who have lower skills or who become more easily disengaged will need major scaffolding from me during this launch phase. So, I stop, and I ask them, "Please list for me the feelings you all have as December approaches." You can imagine the general answers, which mostly fall along the lines of *excited* and *hopeful*. Nearly every answer is in stark contrast to the text, which tells us that Jonas feels "frightened" as December approaches. Thus begins a discussion of *why* he might feel that way. Students posit, "Maybe something terrible happened in his life in December and bad memories come back! Maybe *this* December something bad is going to happen to Jonas or his family, and he knows it's coming but can't stop it. Maybe his family is moving!" Kids begin shouting out many answers, and I allow it.

I then say to them, "Now, as I continue reading, I want you listening for *other* ways that Jonas, his family, or the community where he lives seem very different from ours. I'll stop again soon, and we'll see what you've discovered." I have now provided a purpose for their listening—a scaffold has been built to assist my readers in accessing a story where most of their prior knowledge about the way the world works is useless. They have to acquire a whole new bank of knowledge; there's a whole new set of rules to learn about Jonas's community and the way they live. As master of the text, I know this, but my students don't. Without my planned stopping points throughout the opening chapters, during which time I continue building the scaffold, I would lose many students. We'd never reach the place where the entire class was begging for more if I was not both intentional and strategic in planning for the launch of this read-aloud.

Here is where some elementary teachers may have an advantage. By having much more time with the students, teachers in the elementary grades can adjust the daily schedule, as I always did, during the launch of a book. For example, if my fourth-grade routine was a twenty-minute read-aloud time directly before lunch, I would adjust that during the launching of a historical fiction title such as *The True Confessions of Charlotte Doyle* (Avi 1990). We might have read-aloud time for fifteen minutes first thing in the morning, fifteen more before lunch, fifteen again after lunch, and fifteen more before the final bell. I would plan extra time for not only the reading, but for that important discussion piece so that I could draw the students in and captivate them. Once I had secured their interest, I could return to my regular time slot of twenty minutes a day before lunch. How long the launch takes—how many days or periods of time—depends entirely on the genre and the specific story. My goal here is not to provide you with some type of failsafe number; rather, it is to heighten your awareness that there are many key considerations to successfully launching a read-aloud—far more than some teachers consider.

As a middle school teacher, I routinely read aloud for fifteen to twenty minutes, three times per week. Remember, I had nearly ninety minutes every day. (Did I mention that that's the way God intended language arts to be taught? That's an uninterrupted ninety minutes, too, for those of you taking notes. And may I *just* point out that no one asks teachers to cover both math and science in forty-five minutes, but reading and writing—well, sure, that's easy! Okay, I'm finished. I'm finished. For now.) My students knew they could count on that fifteen to twenty minutes of read-aloud three days a week, and boy, did they keep track of it!

Now, if I were launching a new novel that was realistic fiction, such as Gordon Korman's hilarious *Ungifted* (2012), I'd stick to my routine read-aloud time, because my students' prior knowledge would be sufficient. But if I was reading a multicultural title such as *Shabanu* (Staples 1989), I would probably give over a full forty-five-minute period at least two days in a row just to draw my students into a story set in a different land where entirely different cultural beliefs might be at play compared with those of many of my students. I wouldn't move back to my regular read-aloud schedule until I felt I had captivated the entire group. Launching *Shabanu* requires different planning and execution than launching *Ungifted*.

This is always my advice to content teachers: you can actually give over very little time to read-alouds and still have great success as long as you are careful about the launch of lengthier titles and mindful of the genre. I have had some exciting e-mails from high school math and science teachers telling me they have kids who can't wait to get to class because these teachers are sharing some great stories—and they are reading for only the first five minutes after the bell! Perhaps they offer their students a treat: just a little more time for read-aloud before the period ends *if* the group is working hard all period long, but no promises! The key, these teachers have learned, is that with certain genres they may have to give an entire forty-five-minute math class (or two) over to launching the read-aloud—but then the five minutes a day will be successful, because the students will all be captivated. Some high school department chairperson passed out just now; somebody get the smelling salts. A whole precious period given over to reading aloud? Really? Yes. Quite simply, yes. Need I make a list of all the other times during a school year that we give over a whole period of class time, or even more than one, to "rewards" such as movies, class trips, carnivals, assemblies, and so on? In some of these cases, the issue of educational merit could appropriately be called into question. In the case of launching a read-aloud, it's all about education—it's simply not conventional in the eyes of some people for the chemistry teacher to be the one doing it. Let's remember, that doesn't make it the wrong choice; it's all about the pair of lenses through which you happen to be viewing the situation.

In addition to planning a significant amount of time to successfully launch a lengthier text and being considerate of the genre, teachers must be cognizant of what *day* they choose to begin the launch sequence. Friday, for example, is a terrible day to begin launching a new title: the story is not sustained because of the weekend break. It is always best to launch a book when you have several days in a row to gain momentum with the story before having any days off. Likewise, though your daily routine may not always include a read-aloud, it is wise to read every day when you are launching one (particularly if the genre is demanding) until you have achieved the goal of drawing in every student. Remember, once they're hooked, you can adjust your read-aloud time according to the needs and demands of your own particular grade level and teaching situation.

During a Read-Aloud

Once the read-aloud is successfully launched, you need to keep it moving along. Whatever the schedule becomes, be sure it is something your students can count on. In other words, don't make them "earn it." Keep in mind, too, that long school vacations in the middle of a read-aloud can lead to ruin. Again, this is all about solid planning on your part—you don't allow this to happen, because you have mapped out a plan in advance to be sure you finish the story three full days before the holiday break. (Why punish the kids whose parents remove them from school a day or two early for the break by setting it up so they miss the end and the discussion? It's bound to happen, so let's plan for it by finishing the book three days before the break.)

A lot of significant instruction takes place during a read-aloud. There's been a lot written, for example, about visualization in recent years, and this is a key component of strong reading pedagogy. Kids need to learn to "see the movie in their minds." They need to understand that this is what happens in the minds of good readers: they are watching a movie in their minds as they read. A fine way to deliver that lesson is to stop at preselected moments in a read-aloud (highly descriptive passages of action work best) and ask the students, "Boys and girls—ladies and gentlemen—are you seeing this all happening in your mind? Is the movie playing for you?" Commonplace in my classroom was calling forward students who were willing to "show" us the movie they were watching as we read by acting it out for us. For many years, I taught a unit on high fantasy novels to fifth and sixth graders. My read-aloud to open this unit was Lloyd Alexander's classic novel *The Book of Three* (1964). Taran, an assistant pig-keeper barely on the threshold of manhood, dreams of being a hero but is resigned to his fate working on a farm. In a scene early in the story, the boy brandishes a poker he has been using in his work making horseshoes and uses it as a sword to demonstrate his heroic prowess. The text describes him "slashing at the air and dancing back and forth over the hard-packed earthen floor" (4). What a great visual image! I routinely asked students to volunteer to step forward and "show us how this looked in your mind as I was reading it aloud." Having several students act it out made three things clear to my entire class: (1) Many people in this classroom *are* visualizing what's happening in the book. (2) This is what the teacher means when he talks with us about how reading is watching a movie in your mind. (3) Everyone's movie can be different. It is critical not only to give the message to students that good readers strive to visualize as they read, but to allow them to see frequent modeling of how it is happening in the minds of their peers. Obviously, the teacher can model this as well—but I think it's much stronger, in this case, when it comes from their peer group.

Reading skills can be effectively introduced and/or reinforced through read-alouds (Layne 2009). Remember that every time your teacher instinct (your own incredible superpower) tells you to stop reading aloud and ask a question, there is a reading skill tied to that question. Ask yourself, *What is the skill that's tied to the question I am about to pose?* Then point this out to your students. When Gooney Bird Greene (Lowry 2002) arrives at Watertower Elementary School in Mrs. Pidgeon's second-grade classroom, she "appeared there all alone, without even a mother to introduce her. She was wearing pajamas and cowboy boots and was holding a dictionary and a lunch box" (1). I would be inclined to stop and ask students to tell me what this introduction of Gooney on the very first page of the book has them thinking about her. The reading skill would be inference: the students would use clues from the text, such as Gooney's apparel, as well as what they know about real life—most new kids don't show up without a parent, and wearing pajamas—to make inferences about Gooney and her life.

As we tease out the discussion, I will point out to the students exactly what they are doing: story clues + real life = making inferences. Those inferences may be right or they may be wrong—students will have to read more to find out if they are correct. The opportunity to reinforce reading skills applies to every grade level and every type of text. Think about skills such as main idea or sequencing; they can easily apply to many of the questions that great teachers automatically think to ask when they are reading aloud. Tying the question to the actual reading skill simply takes it a step beyond what we may typically think to do.

When Matt finds himself pointing a gun at his own mother in *The Rules of Survival* (Werlin 2006), I say to ninth-grade students, "How on earth did Matt get into this situation? Somebody retrace the steps that brought him to this moment." The answer, of course, is a series of escalating and dangerous encounters with one of the most terrifying characters ever created in literature. What I am *really* asking of these ninth graders is to sequence—that's the skill needed. Understanding the correct sequence helps us understand this climactic moment in the story. I am going to point out that it is, in fact, the skill of sequencing that helps us evaluate the situation more objectively. This is real teaching—pointing out to the students that someone simply happening upon this situation might believe that Matt is the one who is crazy; however, if you know the sequence of events that led him to this moment, your comprehension of the situation is quite different.

The next step is to take that conversation into real life, reminding students that every sensational story they hear on the news or see happening in the school hallway has a sequence of events behind it. Until you know the whole story, you really don't know the story at all. Every stopping point is a secret reading-skill-reinforcement lesson just waiting to happen. If you stop for only a brief discussion and avoid writing on the whiteboard or getting out the workbooks, the students will never even know you were introducing or reinforcing a skill!

One of the most common questions I have received over the years about read-aloud time has to do with behavior problems. I can speak only from my own experience, which has been consistent. When I pick the right book for the class I am teaching, launch it well, and move it forward in a steady manner, it is very unusual to have to stop reading and deal with a behavior problem. On the rare occasion that it happens, I simply invite the offender out in the hall for a chat. The chat morphs in tone and word choice, depending upon the grade level; however, the message is the same, and it is this: "Read-aloud time is instruction. You engaged in a behavior [poking Purab, pulling Tia's hair, breathing too loud] that interrupted my instruction. This cannot happen again. Should it happen again, you will be disinvited from our read-aloud time for the remainder of this book, and I will find something to occupy your time that shall help you to remember my name all of the days of your life." I have never had a second chat with the same individual, so I cannot speak to that. I am not trying to oversimplify situations that some teachers may be facing. You may have a student in your classroom who has a severe but undiagnosed behavior disorder, or you might have a student who just moved to the United States from a country where she's never heard a word of English, and so on, and all of these factors can play a part. But if you're reading a professional book, you're the kind of educator who'll find a way to resolve this situation. There's no secret cure. I believe, though, that a good book read well alleviates many potential problems.

A word to our late-grade middle and high school teachers: You may well have students balk at being read to if they have been unaccustomed to it in recent years. Do not let them intimidate you. There is a reason you are the trained adult—you know best. You *will* successfully "turn" them, but it may take some time. They may need to act all "big man on campus" about it at first. Just smile and say, "There's a kindergarten teacher in me somewhere looking for an outlet, guys." Then, open with something that will put them on the edge of their seats in a nanosecond. It's all about being strategic!

Concluding a Read-Aloud

A considerable amount of work is put into launching a read-aloud effectively and in keeping things moving throughout the journey, but what about the ending? I strongly encourage teachers to plan, plan, plan for the end. It must be fabulous and uninterrupted by the bell, the principal, the president, or the Pope. I'll never forget giving a seminar in Ohio a few years ago when a woman in the audience raised her hand and asked if I thought it was okay that she had a substitute teacher back in her building ending *The Giver* so she could come and spend a day with me. I smiled politely and said something gracious, but I wanted to say, "What do you *mean* they're ending *The Giver* with a sub? If you're being hospitalized long term, okay. If you're giving an emergency kidney donation to your child, okay. But to spend a day with me—no. I'm not worth it; no one is. I'm not even sure a chat with Lois Lowry herself, one-on-one at the local coffee shop, would be worth letting a sub end that book with your class."

Teachers, we can't make the case that reading aloud *is* instruction and then scoot out at the culmination of all our work. How can someone who hasn't been on the trip lead a discussion about the vacation? When we finish a book, it's time to sigh, it's time to think, and it's time to talk—we must teach kids to do this and model it with them. We should be posing questions such as "Why do you think the author wrote this book?" and "Did we see growth in the main character throughout the story?" and "What secondary character do you see as critical to this story?" We don't want to read the last word on the last page, glance at the clock, and be forced to say, "Third grade, line up for music! We'll talk about the end later this afternoon." I have a news flash for you: it won't be the same later that afternoon. The heat of the moment happens only once, and great instructors are ready for it to happen—they plan meticulously for it as they do for all the great instructional moments they can anticipate.

Back to my earlier example for secondary folks who are locked into that time crunch: treat the ending like the beginning. Once you have successfully launched, you may be moving along only a little at a time, but don't *end* that way! End with a full period—with lots of time to read and lots more to discuss. It's the only way to do it right.

Canceling a Read-Aloud

I need to say a word here about canceling read-aloud time, because it's a deadly decision, in my book (that's a great pun, by the way). Ever had a flight canceled? The arrival of a new puppy put off another day? How about your dream date falling apart at the eleventh hour? (Pennie Allgood, if you're reading this, I don't believe for *one minute* that you had a rescheduled dental appointment at 6:30 p.m. on that Saturday night back in '77.) When something you're looking forward to is canceled, the disappointment is palpable. There can be a tendency to cancel read-aloud time when you get behind. My advice is—don't. Once you start giving that message, you become unreliable, and students will not give themselves over fully to read-aloud time anymore for fear of disappointment. Canceling read-aloud time also sends the message that it is not important or not "as" important as "real instruction." If you really believed that, you wouldn't be reading this book.

One key benefit of a consistent read-aloud time is that kids enjoy being with text; this affects attitude, and attitude precedes action. Kids don't take books home and read if they never have any pleasant experiences with books. In a world that is busier and busier, we need to be very mindful of just how important it is for our students to have some positive and enjoyable experiences with text. When they arrive in your class nearly salivating to hear more of a book you've been delivering so well, and you cancel on them, it's grounds for mutiny. We all have "those days" when we realize far too late that our best-laid plans are disastrous, and we're running out of time. The inclination for some of you will be to cancel the read-aloud time under such circumstances, and I'm begging you not to do it. Better yet, if something has to go on a given day, ask the students whether it should be their read-aloud time or something else. We already know what they'll say, don't we? And I ask you, what is the message underscoring their response?

FAQs

Over the years, I have received a lot of letters and e-mails filled to overflowing with questions about read-aloud time. The best questions come up again and again; that's how I know they're good ones. Some of these inquiries have left me laughing out loud, and others have given me a lot to ponder. To keep you engaged, I've taken the liberty of merging the content of much of this mail into a series of queries and responses à la "Dear Abby," but with very little tweaking—you are indeed reading from my mail.

Dear Steven,
I am at my wits' end! My students keep running out and getting their own copies of the book I am reading aloud. Then they read ahead! I am so frustrated. How can I keep them from getting their hands on these books? Please help.

Sincerely,
Witless in Walla Walla

Dear Witless,
You have me laughing out loud, you nut! I think you may have forgotten about one of the chief goals of reading aloud to your students: to get them excited about books! The problem you are encountering has happened because you are obviously picking great books and reading them terribly well. It appears to me that you are, in fact, filled to overflowing with "wits." Perhaps you just became distracted by something shiny for

a moment. Come back to us. You are a star; the evidence is clear on that matter.

Laughing aloud,

Steven

Witless's issue is an important one, and often what is at the heart of the teacher's complaint is that a student got his hands on a copy of the book, read ahead, and then blabbed—ruining the ending for others. Or better yet, this student will "predict" the entire next three chapters of events when called on (which is how the teacher figures out that the guilty party has, in fact, read ahead). These are real-life teaching situations that need some thought. My advice is to tell the students up front that you already know many of them are going to fall in love with the books you share during read-aloud time. Hence, there must be an understanding. Anyone who loves the book *so much* that she talks her mom into buying it for her or checks a copy out of the library may surely read ahead. *But*, that same person must not insult the teacher's intelligence by "predicting" in front of the entire class what she already knows to be true or by spoiling any of the story for those who have not read ahead. Either of those behaviors interferes with instruction. Any behavior interfering with instruction is grounds for a serious chat. I personally see no difference between taking three friends into the bathroom and telling them what's going to happen when Howard Jeeter meets Molly Vera Thompson for the first time in *The Kid in the Red Jacket* (Park 1987) and firing off a BB gun in my classroom. Both behaviors interfere with my ability to instruct the students according to my plan. It's amazing how easily kids can really understand that when you explain it to them. I always made a pact with my classes that they could read ahead all they wanted, as long as they didn't allow their new knowledge to interfere with my instruction. Over the years I can think of only once when it wasn't honored by a student. Sadly, he was never seen or heard from again.

Dear Steven,

We have the most amazing book room in my school! I actually designed it my-self—not that it matters—but I did. I'm sure you're very busy with your own family and career, but I have attached twenty-seven photos of my book room in case you have time to view them. When you were in Anchorage at our conference, I went to your session but did not have time to ask this question before rushing off to Mem Fox's luncheon (she was fabulous, by the way!). When I am reading aloud The Tale of Despereaux (DiCamillo 2003) with my teammate Harold (we combine our second-grade classes for this), I keep thinking we should take fifty-two copies of the book from our book room and give them to the kids to make sure they are following along as we read aloud. Harold rarely argues, but he really gets worked up about this issue and says we should leave the books in the book room. I will admit they look really good on the shelves, which are all color coded, by the way, to match my leveling system. Check out photos 5, 12, 23, and 24 to see how it looks! What are your thoughts on the matter?

All the best,
Addled in Anchorage

Dear Addled,
So glad to hear that Mem was fabulous at the conference luncheon. How did I do in my session? If I'm going to have to play long-distance referee between you and Harold, then you must both agree to compromise, because you're both right. We always want to get books into the hands of kids; however, I have come up with an idea that in situations like this, we should let it be their choice whether they follow along or not. So . . . make the books available, but don't force them. Lovin' those photos, yes sirree.

Less than perplexed,
Steven

Addled in Anchorage raises a great issue. Isn't "following along" called for during read-aloud time? Aren't we remiss if we don't insist on it—if we are fortunate enough to have enough copies of the title for every child? It all goes back to the reason behind read-aloud time. One of the chief benefits of reading aloud to kids of any age is to favorably affect their attitudes. Trust me, your students do plenty of following along in school—most of the day, probably. Read-aloud time needs to be enjoyable, and as soon as you force a reluctant reader to hold a book in his hand and follow along, you've set up a strike against yourself. If, however, you have a few copies to make available or even enough for everyone to have one who would like to—and you set those copies out along with your invitation to follow along *at will*—you now have something keen to observe. Will some of your more reluctant readers decide at any point that they *want* to follow along? They might! And don't be discouraged if they do one day and then fail to repeat the behavior.

There can be many reasons why that happens, the first of which has to do with the difficulty of the text (an issue I'll address in Chapter 3). What I love about allowing students the choice of whether or not to follow along is that it puts them in the driver's seat and us in the passenger's seat. Trust me—we'll have the better view.

Dear Steven,

I don't understand why I never hear you talk about putting the students in charge of the read-aloud. I don't mean to seem disrespectful, but I think you're out of touch with real teachers. I wonder if you've forgotten how hard teaching is. I'm tired! I need a lot more breaks than I get in a day! I began putting the kids in charge of my read-alouds years ago, and I get so many papers graded that way. Sometimes I even slip out of the room and grab some snacks in the lounge, and I've never been caught yet!

Yours truly,
Devilish in Durbin

Dear Devilish,

You certainly do have a bit of the devil in you—the same has been said about me on multiple occasions; I trust you'll uncover that from this response. You have never heard me talk about putting kids in charge of read-aloud time because I am not keen on the idea under normal circumstances. Again, much of it goes back to the rationale for having a read-aloud time. Positively affecting attitude is critical during read-aloud time, and for that to happen, you must have a well-prepared, talented, and capable reader. Anyone who's ever witnessed round-robin reading and would describe it as a consistently engaging experience for the listening audience has rowed a little too far from shore and lost both oars. There are certainly instances when kids can and should orally deliver text, but to have it happen routinely during read-aloud time would not be my typical recommendation. As for your positing that I might be out of touch, I find such a query highly entertaining, coming from an educator who's concentrating on grading papers rather than on the story the rest of her leaderless class is experiencing together.

Pitchfork in hand,
Steven

I would like to go on record as saying that Devilish in Durbin was a combination of three e-mails and that each one was, in its singularity, far more biting than this one. Nevertheless, I'm glad someone raised this issue. I think asking anyone to orally read something they have not had adequate time to prepare to read aloud is a big roll of the dice. I'm not saying it should never happen, and I'm not saying it's bad pedagogy in certain situations, but I *am* saying that "proceed with caution" flares should light up when we discuss the issue. If you routinely turn the read-aloud over to the students, you are giving up a massive opportunity to engage the class in critical discourse or to scaffold their reading skills. You have been trained to do this; your students have not. Are there times when it can happen? Yes. Could it be done well? Yes. Do I see it as "the norm" in most cases? No.

Dear Steven,
I love listening to audio-recorded books. They are amazing! I get so much more "read" that way because I listen to them in my car traveling to and from work. On vacation, our entire family listens to at least one book, and sometimes two. How about in the classroom?

Regards,
Tuning In from Tasmania

Dear Tuning,
I am listening to the same station you are regarding the benefits of recorded books. I believe they have many wonderful uses both at home and at school. Replacing the teacher, however, is not one of them, and that is always my caution on the subject. Promise me you won't take yourself out of the read-aloud equation and insert some kind of mechanical device that will read to your students instead, and you and I will stay perfectly in tune.

Don't touch that dial,
Steven

"Boys and girls, let's all gather around the CD player" is not quite the same as "let's all gather around the teacher." Reading aloud to a group of people—of any age—is an intimate act. It creates a bond that can be and often is very powerful. We must not underestimate that. Recorded books—or the voice issuing from them—will never wipe away the tears of a first grader with a skinned knee at recess or pat the shoulder of a distraught tenth grader who stayed after class to say that her parents are divorcing. Only you can do that, and only you can create the magical bond in your classroom (or in each period of your day) with your students that a great read-aloud fosters. I had a wonderful recording of an elderly man reading Robert Frost's "Stopping by Woods on a Snowy Evening" that I never failed to play during my eighth-grade poetry unit. I loved for them to hear it in that old man's voice. I could read it orally, of course, but not as well because of the small number of years I have spent on this earth and my fairly exuberant personality (I was recently likened to Tigger from Winnie the Pooh—on uppers). I would not, however, willingly replace myself permanently during read-aloud time even if someone else did read the book a bit better. That being said, there are usually exceptions. I understand the seventh-grade teacher who says her voice is ragged already at day's end and so she simply cannot read aloud six periods a day and teach as well. She may have to use a recorded book for one or two periods to rest her voice, but I have two strong suggestions for her: (1) She must rotate the periods where students listen to recorded books so that no classes are permanently robbed of her as the reader. (2) When the class listens to a recorded book, she must be right there "in their midst." No paper grading should be happening, nor should anything "additional" be occupying her time. I always close any discussion of this issue with these words: Never underestimate your own value to your students. Nobody else does it better.

Dear Steven,

Manuel always wants to draw during my read-aloud time. Should I allow it? He is in constant motion in my room, so I am thinking that letting him draw will help, but if I allow him to draw, then can everyone draw? It seems like such a big issue that I have just avoided making the decision and keep telling him no. He just paces back and forth in the back of my room while I am reading, and I try to pretend he isn't there. And another thing—what about kids who want to do homework during read-aloud time? Marveena down the hall lets them do their homework whenever she reads aloud—which isn't all that often. Then, when her kids come to me, it's always, "Mrs. Toot-n-Sweet always let us do our homework when she read to us." I would appreciate your feedback.

Best,
Up in the Air in Upland

Dear Up,

If Manuel is in constant motion and is asking to draw, I say not only let Manuel draw, but buy Manuel a sketchbook and an art supply box—anything to keep him from pacing back and forth in the room during read-aloud time.

As for Marveena down the hall, I cannot support her. You will never convince me that a fourth grader working on long-division homework is completing that task while also fully engaging in the story I am reading aloud. Read-aloud time is instruction—no homework at this time. That's my story, and I'm sticking to it.

Well grounded,

Steven

I like Up in the Air's candidness. When that situation arose in one of my classrooms the first time, it was in second grade. I responded to the "May I draw?" query from Roberto with my own question. "Roberto, would you please draw for me the images you see in your mind while I am reading?" He was quite willing to do that. I was not expecting any type of finished drawings, of course, but my idea would, I hoped, keep Roberto engaged with the story. Caldecott Medal winner David Small has personally spoken to me of his need to be sketching a great deal of the time—especially when he is thinking. I actually witnessed him sketching during the conversation portion of a dinner gathering of several authors. David was every bit of the polite conversationalist throughout that meal, but his drawing hand did not rest too much once he was finished eating.

There could be many explanations for Manuel's restlessness as described in that last note, and many folks reading this section of the book already have a thousand theories. If other members of the class ask to draw, but do not really need to draw, they will quickly tire of it when they realize you will require them to do the same thing: sketch the images they see in their minds during the read-aloud. It is more work to do that for the student who doesn't really *need* to do it.

I have a son who loves being read to; when he was younger he could answer any comprehension question or retell any section of any story I read, as long as he had something in his hands to "fidget with" while he listened. It could be jacks, magnets—anything, really. Those hands never stopped moving as he listened to my stories. If I took these small "helps" away, he became very restless, shifting constantly, impatient and unable to focus. I recommend that all teachers make allowances for students who can become fully engaged with a small amount of help from us. These days my son has outgrown that need and can focus on his own, but I wonder what might have happened if I had been unwilling to allow him to use his magnets when he was smaller?

And a word on kids telling you how great they had it with last year's teacher, if I may? I always smiled and said, "Well, yes, last year, you see, you had Mrs. Toot-n-Sweet—the nice teacher—and this year you have me."

∽ Position Statement

Why Reading Aloud Matters

Linda B. Gambrell

Clemson University—South Carolina, USA
Distinguished Professor of Education
International Literacy Association President
2007–2008

There are so many reasons why reading aloud matters. One simple reason that reading aloud in pre-K through college classrooms matters is that the human voice makes words "sing" and books come alive. Hearing beautiful language being read aloud can take you away to another world. Reading aloud to students helps them fall in love with language and books!

A second reason it is important to read aloud in the classroom is that book language is a second language. Consider the following sentences: "When I first saw the pearls, they hung on my own grandmother's neck. When she walked me to school every morning, that necklace glowed in the sunlight." Beautiful language, but no one talks like that! The vocabulary in books doesn't appear in spoken language. The everyday language that students hear does not prepare them to enter into the world of books, because both narrative and informational books represent book language that is very different from spoken language. Our richest and most descriptive language is found in books, and the more experiences students have with teacher read-alouds, the better prepared they are for successfully navigating book language.

Third, reading aloud is a powerful tool for motivating students to read. When students hear a good book, they often want to read it for themselves—or they might search out books by the same author or look for more information on the topic. Teacher read-aloud time allows students to enjoy stories and informational books just for sheer pleasure and to develop knowledge that is important to the topics that are being explored in the classroom. It also allows students access to books that may be appropriate for their age level but that are too difficult for them to read independently.

I have long realized that the central and most important goal of reading instruction is to foster a love of reading. *As teachers, we need to remember that we can teach our students all the skills needed for proficient reading, but if they do not* choose to read—*if they are not* motivated to read—*they will never reach their full literacy potential. Reading aloud plays an important role in helping our students develop a deep love and appreciation for the sheer pleasure of reading.*

Some of my favorite classroom memories are related to reading aloud to my students. I loved giving "voices" to characters, providing sound effects, and acting out scenes from stories. I read science books aloud, and then we would do experiments. We read gardening books and planted flowers outside our window so we could see them bloom. And, in one of the first graduate literacy courses I taught, I learned that reading aloud can be just as powerful in graduate classes. True story—I read aloud the abstract from Dolores Durkin's classic 1978 study "What Classroom Observations Reveal About Reading Comprehension Instruction" to my graduate students and told them that I thought the study would change how we teach reading comprehension and that it was a "must-read." It was not, however, a formal assignment. The following week in class several students had read the study and were so excited about it that we spent much of the class discussing Durkin's paper—something that wasn't even on the syllabus. The power of read-aloud knows no age limit.

My position on reading aloud is that it is one of life's greatest pleasures.

As a teacher, I loved reading aloud to my students. It can't be overestimated in terms of its value to literacy development. Reading aloud deserves to be a high priority in the literacy curriculum.

⟋ Position Statement

Reading Aloud: Shared Pleasure in the Classroom

Henrietta Dombey

University of Brighton—Brighton, England
Professor Emeritus of Literacy in Primary Education
United Kingdom Literacy Association President
2002–2003

Children need to be helped to make written texts come to life in personal ways, to learn how to make the words on the page or the screen speak. Shared pleasure and active mental engagement are what reading aloud has to offer. Learning to read is hard. The battle through the undergrowth of English spelling can make it arduous for children to construct satisfying meaning. They need the help that being read to provides.

Through their experience of hearing stories and poems read aloud, young children in the early years of school extend their experience of language, building on their experience of conversation to include the much more explicit forms and more elaborate meanings of written language. This is achieved not through repeated exercises but through the pleasure of making meaning together. Your voice reveals to the listening children the shape of the text—what is expected and what is surprising and how all the parts hang together. Those who are read to extensively in the early years of school learn to read with more ease and engagement and are better able to understand and predict the texts they later try to read for themselves.

Reading aloud gives older children a relaxation from the tension of completing school tasks and a shared experience of enjoyment, but relaxation and shared pleasure are not the only effects. As you infuse the text with the expressive cadences of your voice, you can give them a sense of the power written text has to allow listeners into others' experiences and emotions as well as others' hopes, pleasures, and terrors; your listeners are transported to other places and other times and given other ways of seeing the world. You also provide the children in your class with a shared frame of reference—a path for taking their understanding forward in company with each other. And you enrich their writing. Children who are read to in class write with more assurance, using a wider range of vocabulary, sentence structures and larger text structures than those denied this experience (Barrs and Cork 2001).

The choice of text matters. Informational texts can, at times, be more difficult to read aloud. The language needs to be resonant and the subject matter gripping. All of the children in the class should be able to make some satisfying sense of the text, but there should be enough meaning potential to reward those more experienced in the language and the meanings of books. And the text should matter to you, too, so that as you read, you are inviting those who are listening to share your pleasure and concern about what the author is saying.

The time of day is important as well. Twenty minutes of being read to at the end of the school day has much to offer children from age seven on up, but the youngest children, the three-to-five-year-olds, need sessions early in the day, when they are not too tired but can make the mental effort to make personal sense of the words they are hearing. For them, each reading should be complete—a whole picture book or sequence of verses. They may want you to immediately reread the text you have just shared with them: repetition has an important part to play in developing a familiarity with the particular rhythms and cadences of written language.

Your voice is what brings the text to life. You don't have to be an A-rated performer, but you do need to use variations in pitch, volume, pauses, and stress to reveal and point up the meaning of the text you read, in this way acting as a model for the "voice in the head" that each child needs to develop. You might also, on occasion, interject a tentative commentary to show how you make sense of the text: "Ah! So he's planning a party, is he?" or

"That's why he didn't want her to take the bus!"

But reading aloud shouldn't just be a solo performance. From the earliest years onward, the children can be invited to speculate about what is going to happen or why a character behaved in a certain way. And, of course, they should be invited to join in with repeated choruses or motifs.

We all know that reading matters—that it can take you far beyond your own firsthand experience and show you other ways of living, other ways of thinking, and other values. We know that reading—pleasurable reading—is threatened by the seductive charms of electronic sounds and images. But if we invest ourselves imaginatively in regular read-aloud sessions, we make the experience of children and young adults with written text both easier and richer.

Chapter 3

Selecting the Appropriate
Read-Aloud

Dear Ms. Werlin,

Teaching freshman English and AP literature and composition at a suburban Chicago high school these past eight years, I've had the opportunity to share countless positive reading experiences with the young people in my classes. Recently, I read your novel *The Rules of Survival* aloud with my freshmen, and doing so has been not only one of the most interesting episodes in my career, but one of the most conversationally productive. I am writing both to express gratitude for the book and to share a little about our experience reading it.

The Rules of Survival is unquestionably the most intense story I've read aloud with freshmen, and although my students have enjoyed works we've read together before, the tenor of their interest in your book has been markedly different. From the moment I began reading the book aloud, a tense and palpable hush pervaded our classroom. Toward the beginning, for example, when Matthew talks back to Nikki after seeming to criticize her spending habits, I paused a few seconds in my reading as Matthew waits to see if his mother will simply accept his apology. As I read, matter-of-factly, the single-word paragraph "no" that guarantees Matt will face Nikki's wrath, the entire class seemed to collectively shrink into their seats. Then, as Nikki strikes Matthew not once but twice, in punishment, a number of students visibly winced, whereas others simply sat as they would for most of the book's subsequent events, mouths slightly agape in utter disbelief.

But I did not choose to read *Rules* aloud simply for shock value. The book raises a number of timely social problems that are made more tangible because you have invoked them through *story*. Throughout our reading, students raised numerous weighty questions, from What rights do parents have when punishing their children? to Why don't adults help the abused? to Will Matt eventually hurt Nikki, and would it be wrong if he did? Discussing such questions outside the context of shared reading would likely be too superficial or uncomfortable for students to benefit from significantly; couched in fiction, however, my students felt free to discuss the all-too-common realities on which the book is based—and, tragically, with which some children must contend daily.

In addition to such moral questions, my classes and I wondered—possibly because we wished these events were entirely fictional—from what sources did you draw inspiration for this book? Having dedicated the work to "the survivors," are you closely connected to such people, and if so, what have they said in reaction to Matt's experiences? And since we're student writers as well as readers, what suggestions could you give us on how to draw meaning, like Matt does, from experience? Your time and thoughts, like your book, are very much appreciated.

With gratitude,
David Alan Smith

High School English Teacher
South Elgin High School
Elgin, Illinois

Dear Mr. Smith,

Thank you for your letter and for letting me share the experience you had in reading The Rules of Survival *with your students. You described it so well that I could almost see your class living the story of Matthew Walsh. It is both satisfying and humbling.*

Few of us know how we would act in the real world if we were in Matt's shoes. But story lets us imagine ourselves there. This can happen when we read a story alone. It happens even more forcefully when we read a story with other people and talk about it. Your experience is proof of that. It's why I love reading fiction so much. I want to understand other people. I want to love them. Books nourish that part of me every bit as much as real life can.

Writing a novel is at its core an extremely private experience. I'm moved that Rules of Survival *caused your class to ask those probing questions about social issues. They were and are important questions for me, too. But I didn't keep questions like that in mind while I worked. In the years I wrote scenes and chapters, and then deleted and rewrote them, over and over, I kept my focus tightly on Matt and imagined myself into his skin. I asked only questions like the following: Is this what he'd really think? Is this what he'd really do? What is the emotional truth-line of the story?*

The question of emotional truth brings me to your questions about inspiration, and about how a student writer might learn to draw meaning and create story from past experience. You may be surprised by what I have to say.

Many readers of Rules of Survival *assume that I must have had an abusive parent myself. Not so; I am fortunate to have had loving, good parents. But at the same time, I am Matthew, and he is me.*

Here is my story: I wrote Rules of Survival *while involved in a dangerous relationship. I did not understand this at the time. Humans are capable of enormous self-delusion in the name of love, or at least, I was. I was a working writer still, however, and I created Matthew and Nikki and their world, and lived there in my head, trying to get at the emotional truth of Matt's story of endurance and survival, of being surrounded only by bad choices, while I was living a similar story of my own that I refused to see truthfully.*

We think of writers choosing with deliberation the stories they want to tell. Not me. I don't write a story because I want to teach it to readers. I write a story to learn it for myself.

All the best,
Nancy Werlin

My pal Ben and I were hanging out several years back. We grabbed some burgers and eventually ended up renting a movie. He was going on and on about this terrific movie that I just *had* to see, so I let him select *Pay It Forward*. I have never been so depressed in all my life! I also can't seem to remember hanging out with Ben again in recent years. How could he say that movie is a good movie? Inspirational—that's what he called it! The movie ends, and I want to throw myself off a cliff while Ben feels *inspired*.

Selecting a great read-aloud is a lot like selecting a great movie—it's all a matter of opinion. Throughout this book, you will find a lot of recommendations for read-alouds, but it is vitally important that you remember that those doing the recommending are speaking from *their* experience, not from yours. Louise Rosenblatt (1938) reminds us that what we bring to the text as readers is an important consideration in the transaction that occurs during the reading process. The meaning on the page has not been brought to life until my life experience as a reader begins to interact with it. Our experiences, beliefs, predispositions, and passions all play a role in how we experience a text, so it would only be natural that we would disagree with one another about which books are great for which grade levels, which titles are better for read-alouds versus which are better for novel studies, and so on. People who recommend read-alouds to you are recommending those particular books because they worked in their classrooms, during a specific year (or multiple years), in the community where they teach. Those three factors play an enormous role in the successful outcome, so you must keep that in mind. I can remember years when I made massive alterations to nearly my entire curriculum despite being in the same grade level, school, and community. Why? Because *this* year's class was clearly a far cry from *last* year's class. Heads are nodding as you read those words, I know. So, as we move into a discussion about selecting a great read-aloud, we need to keep ourselves "professionally aware" of the many factors that can influence the decision to designate a book as such.

Listening Up

Those of you with a clinical background in reading instruction are aware of the difference between listening level and silent reading level. For those who haven't had that training, a landmark review of literature by Sticht and James (1984) provided information on oft-cited studies revealing that the listening level of a child (the level at which he hears and comprehends text) is significantly higher than his silent reading level. The typical rule of thumb is that until the late part of eighth grade, the difference in these two levels for the average reader is about two years. This information is important to consider when selecting a read-aloud, because it reminds us that the average first-grade student can actually comprehend text written at a third-grade level—if it is being read aloud. Consider first graders laughing aloud at a television program for which they could never read the actual written script. How are they comprehending what is happening on that television program if they are incapable of reading the script? It is because their listening level is much higher than their silent reading level. Thus, until the late part of grade eight in particular, my recommendation is that you consider selecting the majority of your read-alouds from texts written one to two grade levels above the grade level you are teaching.

Obviously, you have to use common sense. The third-grade teacher cannot simply select any fifth-grade novel and begin reading it aloud. The content must be appropriate, and the time of year and maturity of the current class must play a factor in your decision as well. For those teaching beyond grade eight but who have a population where the vast majority of the students are reading below grade level, this is still applicable. And even for those teaching in grade eleven with a very high-functioning group of students, it can do no harm to select texts for reading aloud that you feel will have your students "reaching" a bit in terms of theme, vocabulary, and content.

It is my belief that critics of read-aloud time are, for the most part, uneducated with regard to the benefits available to students who are "listening up" in classrooms. When the text selected for read-aloud time has students "listening up" one to two grade levels, teachers become the medium for exposing those students to more mature vocabulary, more complex literary devices, and more sophisticated sentence structures than they would be finding in the grade-level texts they could navigate on their own. Last time I checked, this was called excellent teaching! With teachers as the conduit, students are able to enjoy a much richer experience than would otherwise be available to them. Exposure to these higher-level texts, as long as they are content appropriate, is in my mind a significant "upgrade" for them, and politicians, parents, and administrators should be thrilled with any teachers who are providing this opportunity—and who can articulate why they are doing so.

I have scared a few people with those last few paragraphs, I imagine. Some of our primary teachers are now worrying that I might be suggesting they stop reading most or all of those terrific picture books. The upper-grade teachers and librarians who are "professionally aware" read aloud from picture books a lot, too, so now they are worried as well. And then there are those who have some titles they have read aloud every year since the dawn of time, the beloved books they could almost read aloud without the text in hand—and though those treasured titles *are* chapter books, they are *not* above grade level enough to truly count as "listening up" books. And to all of these groups of anxiety-ridden educators I say, "All things in moderation."

The most important issue in all of this is that you become articulate educators who have rationale for why, when, where, and how you do what you do. There are a million writing lessons inside every picture book. Of course, you'll still read them aloud. Picture books are a highly valuable tool in every grade level; sometimes we know that our students need what I call "a chat," and a picture book can set the mood, foreshadowing the topic of our chat that is likely to have something to do with poor choices being made by someone in our room—and I am rarely the guilty party. In addition, the entertainment value of picture books should be recognized; we want to read them because they're just fun. We have seven minutes until the bell, and *Have I Got a Book for You* (Watt 2009) is going to make us laugh—let's enjoy it. Though the issue of having kids "listen up" is important, I want to reinforce my love for great picture book read-alouds by sharing a few favorites.

- ✸ **Beaumont, Karen.** Beaumont is nothing short of a sheer genius with words, and *I Ain't Gonna Paint No More!* begs for a prediction, page after page, from any child . . . or adult in the room.

- ✸ **Beaumont, Karen.** Two in a row—I know, I know—but I said she was a genius. *Who Ate All the Cookie Dough?* is a pattern book that breaks the pattern in a unique way and then rewards us with a wonderful surprise ending.

- ✸ **Casanova, Mary.** I love cumulative books—especially when you have no idea from the title that they *are* cumulative books. When they're drawn by Ard Hoyt and when Casanova gives you a lovely ending, sweet satisfaction is always the result. I'd try to steal away in this *One-Dog Canoe* any day.

✤ **Haseley, Dennis.** The first time I read *A Story for Bear*, I bought seven hardcover copies. I would do it again today. I tell my students it is the perfect match of a writer and an illustrator; the fact that the actual theme underscores the power of reading aloud is a considerable bonus.

✤ **Henkes, Kevin.** The favored teacher's fall from grace has not been written about nearly enough, from my point of view. Of course, after reading Henkes's masterful and hysterical *Lilly's Purple Plastic Purse,* who'd be foolish enough to try?

✤ **LaRochelle, David.** *The Best Pet of All* is a delightful take on a clever hero's quest to conquer his tyrannical mother's position on a family dog. He wins in the end. The retro art adds to the fun.

✤ **MacLachlan, Patricia.** One of the most perfect picture books ever created is, without question, McLachlan's soul-stirring *All the Places to Love.* Listening to it read orally by a skilled reader is a gift in every sense of the word. When I read this book aloud, I always come away feeling that I've lost something, we've lost something . . . and I want us all to find it again.

✤ **Teague, Mark.** There's great fun in picture books with sophisticated humor. *Dear Mrs. LaRue: Letters from Obedience School* hit the mark and had my middle schoolers in stitches the first time I read it aloud. Our upcoming letter-writing unit was suddenly signed, sealed . . . and delivered.

✤ **Tobias, Tobi.** I keep a copy of *Serendipity* at both home and work; I used to travel with one until I lent it out while on the road and it never came back. Reading this book aloud is guaranteed to make everyone of every age in any room smile—and mean it.

✤ **Van Allsburg, Chris.** Failing to read aloud *The Polar Express* annually should result in coal in your stocking. If you know this title, I don't need to say any more. If you don't know this title, what have you been doing with all of your free time? Get to the bookstore, pronto! I still hear the bell, and I hope you do, too.

Wilson, Karma. *Moose Tracks* should be read aloud while enjoying ice cream of the same name. The book has not only amazing rhyme and rhythm (a Karma Wilson trademark), but also an attribute that very few picture books can claim: a mystery at its center that needs to be solved!

 Woodson, Jacqueline. This incredible story of the racial tension dividing a town is told in a lyrical, hopeful voice as two young girls dare to do what no one else has even considered. *The Other Side* packs an understated message into a beautiful package; it's one to read aloud again and again.

As with picture books, chapter books can contain a life lesson that is exactly what's needed in your fourth-grade classroom—so at times you're reading the chapter book *Skinnybones* (Park 1982) aloud, despite the fact that most of your fourth graders could read it on their own. I understand that; it's going to happen, and there's nothing wrong with it at all. That being said, I want to encourage you as a professional to do what I call "trolling and doling." I want you to *troll* through the library of your typical read-alouds and *dole* out some teacher tough love to yourself. How many of those titles are genuinely stretching your students? Are your kids listening up *most* of the time? It's not my job to tell you how often they should be listening up or how often you want them listening up. The answer to that should come from the stimulating professional dialogue that can be found at each and every faculty meeting in your building as you address the matters that will change the lives of children for all eternity. Or, you could talk it up and make a decision with a pal standing in line in the photocopy room, which might be as professionally stimulating as the dialogue in your building gets (but I hope for better!).

Considering the Genre

I spoke about teacher tough love a moment ago. Well, we're heading back that way again, and this time it could be really hard on you. Some of you may need to stop reading this riveting professional commentary for a few minutes and do some stress breathing or take an antidepressant before sojourning onward. The reason is that you might be a *genre-hater*; in fact, my money is on the fact that a lot of you are, because most normal people are. They try to hide it, of course, but they know the truth. I was one for a long time. I'm recovering now, though. I hope you will seek recovery, too, if you know you need help.

Genre-haters have decided there are certain genres of literature they can live with-out. They may have amassed a host of reasons that keep them from being anywhere near the genres they abhor, and yet they can be great lovers of books and sincere and success-ful reading motivators. My concern about all of this as it relates to read-alouds is this: if you loathe a specific genre, you're likely to avoid it when selecting your read-alouds. Now, that's all well and good for you and all the students in the class who are just like you, but what about those who are not at all like you? They get nothing? So Hortense, who is a fantasy freak and loves dragons and trolls and characters named Eucalaytalya, will not hear a single fantasy story read aloud all year because you, her teacher, hate high fantasy stories? For *shame*, I say! It's nothing short of an absolute abuse of your power, and we are going to have a chat about this right now. We became teachers to put kids first—not ourselves. If you want to put yourself first, work in the government, not in our schools.

I mentioned earlier that read-aloud time is an intimate time; it does a lot of good in terms of building community. My caution is that sometimes the community can look a little lopsided because well-meaning teachers have organized a terrific group of books to be read aloud without realizing that they are all (or mostly) from the same genre. That's like telling the class, "All of you who love the same kind of books as I do are going to have an amazing year. The rest of you, oh, well." Not one of us would ever speak those words to kids, but do our *actions* send that message?

I am a big proponent of vow making, and an even bigger proponent of vow keeping. I love the word *vow*, in fact. We don't use it enough; let's get on that. Now, how about if you vow to read aloud from every genre to your class(es) next year? Would you do it? For me? Pretty please? I'm not talking about one of those silent-vow deals, either. I'm talking about a spoken vow that you make to your classes and ask to be held accountable for by the students. (Readership in this book would have just dropped by 72 percent if you weren't the brilliant professionals I know you to be.) Even the most professional educators can become a tad cranky when professional books suggest they change some-thing sacred or, even worse, do something new that is an uncomfortable stretch. I know, I know. But this is the better way, readers. It just is.

For those of you willing to go there, I'm so proud! Gold stars all around, but I've also got to get you some help. If you're a historical fiction–hater, we have to find you a historical fiction chapter book or novel that you can stomach. Where will you look for help? I point you in the direction of a terrific librarian and also in the direction of your past and current students who declare themselves lovers of the genre you "avoid." We won't use the word *hate* anymore; you're past it. We also won't tell the kids about your past prejudicial tendencies; this is the new you—on the road to recovery! You may find, as I have, that when the kids love the experience you are providing by reading this genre aloud, you start saying to yourself, *Well, it's not all that bad.* Seeing the students enjoying the book just has that effect on you—you big softie. I'm going to be very proud of every one of you who goes after this issue hard, and I hope you will share your great success stories with me and, more important, with your colleagues. This, teachers, is in my mind what real professional development and growth looks like! We confront a truth that we know is getting in the way of our reaching all the kids, and we take action. Doesn't that say more about the kind of teacher you are striving to be than having someone watch you teach a forty-one-minute lesson once a year? I've said it before—the system is flawed.

Including Nonfiction

I am *not* Mr. Nonfiction, and I never pretend to be what I am not; it's a bad plan all the way around. Now, don't misunderstand my comment; I'm not a genre-hater, but growing up I was one. Now, I have a very healthy respect for nonfiction text, and I think it is critically important that our kids receive exposure to it and that they learn to read and comprehend it well. It's just that, personally, I have always been drawn to fiction, whereas my wife runs straight for the nonfiction section of the bookstore. That said, I have made a conscious effort throughout my career to be intentional about walking over to the nonfiction section of the library or the bookstore and selecting or purchasing nonfiction texts to read. I've read a great many wonderful nonfiction books this way—but only because of my deep desire to grow myself as a reader and so that I can model the same for my students.

There's been a lot written since the Common Core State Standards were released about time spent on narrative versus expository text. Some well-intended but not-so-well-informed individuals have misread the memo and are running about, telling the language arts people to cut all narrative or practically all narrative text out of instruction so we can be sure kids are focusing on expository text. Nonfiction will, of course, represent the bulk of that in most cases.

We would do well to remember that our students are getting a healthy dose of non-fiction/expository text in all or almost every subject area outside of the English language arts. Now, stop right here a minute. Please don't go running down the corridor screaming, "Barbara! Steven Layne says it's okay for us to use only narrative text because all the other subject areas are doing expository for us!" That is *not* in any way what Steven Layne is saying . . . keep reading. What students might *not* be getting in those other subject areas is assistance in learning to navigate that nonfiction text, training in identifying textual features, and opportunities to preview, predict, and read for confirmation or modification of their thinking. Thus, the English language arts folks have a duty to "do our thing" with nonfiction—and that includes read-alouds.

The sad truth is, we aren't. A significant study by Yopp and Yopp (2006) found that even in the primary grades (pre-K through grade three) where nonfiction text is abundantly available, teachers rarely read informational text aloud to the children. A landmark and oft-cited study by Duke (2000) revealed that on average only 3.6 minutes per day were spent with informational text in the first-grade classrooms where her research was conducted. Similarly, an analysis of two different instructional reading series (Moss 2008) found limited exposure to nonfiction text in the materials available for grades one through three; let's hope there has been significant change since these studies were conducted. I'm not sure it is (or was) an issue only in the primary grades, either. I did a quick survey of forty self-proclaimed "read-aloud" upper-grade teachers (grades six through twelve) at a seminar just four weeks ago about how many use nonfiction. The response: one. Although it's a far cry from an empirical study, it's not encouraging. Linda Hoyt would have a stroke.

A 2014 article in *The Reading Teacher* by Tony Stead delivers one of the best-written and most compelling arguments I have read for the inclusion of the nonfiction read-aloud in particular. I want everyone to read that article cover to cover straightaway. Get moving, now, and order it or download it or do whatever you need to do to be sure you're going to get it before you forget and become distracted by something. Stead's position, that nonfiction literature allows an opportunity for many students to bring prior knowledge to the table and become contributors rather than "passively waiting to hear a story unfold" (488), is noteworthy. In fact, I thought he made that point so well, I was inclined to stop three people on the street and mention it.

I recently had some teachers of young children tell me they did not think their students would enjoy nonfiction read-alouds; in fact, they were sure their students preferred "stories." Maybe they were right, or maybe it was the teachers themselves who preferred the stories. When given the choice, the children participating in an interesting study by Kletzien and Szabo (1998) chose nonfiction titles *over* narrative nearly half the time. That information should, at the very least, give us pause. I think it's also important to consider that depending on the design and text structure of a nonfiction book as well as the grade level and listening stamina of our students, we may not always be reading the entire book aloud—and that's okay.

It could be that teachers who have not intentionally included nonfiction titles in their read-aloud programs will find Stead's article to be a much-needed "wake-up call." He goes on to explain that more than 98 percent of the teachers he works with acknowledged that they do not use enough nonfiction text for read-aloud purposes. In fact, many teachers he spoke with (75 percent) didn't know how to locate nonfiction materials to read to their children. In such cases, may I suggest turning to the Orbis Pictus Award lists found on the National Council of Teachers of English website. The NCTE Orbis Pictus Award was established in 1989 for promoting and recognizing excellence in the writing of nonfiction for children, and the annual lists of these tremendous books are available and easily found on the site. Likewise, the American Library Association's Robert F. Sibert Informational Book Medal and Honor Book Awards, presented annually since 2001, are given to honor the authors, illustrators, and/or photographers of the most distinguished informational books published for children in the preceding year. These award-winning titles are easily found on the ALA website. And let us not forget the ILA's fabulous Choices lists. The International Literacy Association (formerly the International Reading Association) annually releases booklists that are sure to contain some important nonfiction titles. I especially care about these lists because the books that are on them are chosen by the kids (Children's Choices and Young Adult Choices) or by their teachers (Teachers' Choices) rather than by an adult-only awards panel that is sometimes heavily populated by people who do not necessarily work with kids or teens on a regular basis. The Choices lists are easily found at www.reading.org. Stead's article also offers two great suggestions for finding strong nonfiction reads: Dorfman and Cappelli's *Nonfiction Mentor Texts* (2009) and the popular Goodreads website (www.goodreads.com/shelf/show/kids-non-fiction). And then, there's yours truly. I decided to share five great nonfiction read-alouds that became ten, then fifteen, and finally twenty. I couldn't let you down! I'm separating them into K–3, 4–6, 7–9, and 10–12 lists; however, you know the drill. Only *you* know your community, your parents, your school, and your kids—each year. So, read these books first, and decide what *you* think about incorporating them as read-alouds. I have great faith in your decisions.

Grades K–Three

❋ **Berger, Melvin and Gilda.** Scholastic's True or False series is amazing. *Dangerous Animals* is just one of the many titles in this series that is sure to delight.

❋ **Bishop, Nic.** Nic's wonderful photographs and interesting text are guaranteed to elicit squeals of excitement. *Snakes* will always be a winner, but he has plenty of other terrific titles in his series from which to choose.

❋ **Buckley, Carol.** *Tarra and Bella: The Elephant and Dog Who Became Friends . . .* Really? You don't have to say anything but the title to sell this to little kids. Truly, you don't have to say anything else to sell this to anyone!

❋ **Ehlert, Lois.** The amazing Lois Ehlert decides to share about her life and her artwork. Of course, she gears the book toward her beloved audience of primary readers in *The Scraps Book: Notes from a Colorful Life*.

❋ **Pinborough, Jan.** Won't your kids be shocked to learn that in the early days children were not allowed to check out books? In fact, they were not even allowed inside many libraries. Enter Anne Carroll Moore—*Miss Moore Thought Otherwise*.

Grades Four–Six

❋ **Floca, Brian.** The opening of the transcontinental railroad was life-changing for people in the United States. Do we get that? I'm not sure. Thankfully, we now have *Locomotive* to make it clear.

❋ **Kalman, Maira.** The finest book I've read to deal with 9/11 in a sensitive manner is *Fireboat: The Heroic Adventures of the John J. Harvey*. I'd use it with any grade level. Its inclusion as nonfiction could be questioned, because it is "based on a true story," but I want it in here.

❀ **Murphy, Jim.** *The Great Fire* of 1871 was one of the most colossal disasters in history at that time, leaving nearly 100,000 people suddenly homeless in Chicago. Many thought the Windy City would never recover.

❀ **Sheinkin, Steve.** Counterfeiters, the Secret Service, grave robbers, and Abraham Lincoln. What's not to like? *Lincoln's Grave Robbers* required extensive research; the result is a fast-paced book that reads like a crime drama.

❀ **Truss, Lynn.** Truss's series of picture books on punctuation are great fun and entirely educational. *Twenty-Odd Ducks: Why Every Punctuation Mark Counts!* reinforces the various ways many of these marks assist readers.

Grades Seven–Nine

❀ **Covey, Sean.** I know he doesn't need the exposure, but Covey writes books that connect. *The 6 Most Important Decisions You'll Ever Make* is a guide for teens, and I think we should celebrate any kid who's caught reading it!

❀ **Nancy, Ted.** Do you like to laugh—loudly? *Letters from a Nut* will deliver the chuckles in spades as we read about how the customer service managers of major businesses respond when they receive some outrageous letters.

❀ **Nelson, Pete.** Hunter Scott's history fair project becomes the impetus that clears the name of the captain of the USS *Indianapolis* who became the scapegoat in a navy disaster. *Left for Dead* is an inspirational, true story.

❀ **Sheinkin, Steve.** *Bomb: The Race to Build—and Steal—the World's Most Dangerous Weapon* is just as exciting as the title sounds. Sheinkin has made a name for himself writing gripping nonfiction; this book is a fine example.

❀ **Walker, Sally.** It's hard to imagine an explosion before the A-bomb doing the kind of damage we hear about in *Blizzard of Glass: The Halifax Explosion of 1917* . . . until you read about it. Two thousand lives gone in an instant.

Grades Ten–Twelve

❋ **Beah, Ishmael.** Estimates place the number of children being drugged and/or brainwashed to become soldiers in war-torn lands at nearly 300,000. *A Long Way Gone: Memoirs of a Boy Soldier* allows us to meet one of them.

❋ **Beamer, Lisa.** Two immortal words heard over and over in the days that followed 9/11 were used to title this amazing read: *Let's Roll!* With both candor and grace, the widow of United Flight 93 passenger Todd Beamer models how to move forward after suffering unimaginable loss.

❋ **Burch, Jennings Michael.** Burch redefines *heart wrenching* in *They Cage the Animals at Night.* This autobiography of an abandoned eight-year-old has the power of a Dickens novel . . . with a triumphant ending.

❋ **Earl, Esther.** If John Green's *The Fault in Our Stars* has taken your world by storm, make it a text set by allowing the authentic voice of heroine Esther Earl to provide insight into how to live while you are dying in *This Star Won't Go Out.*

❋ **Haney, Eric.** Developed in the 1970s, Delta Force is an elite Special Forces unit about which very little has ever been made public. Haney, as a founding member, is surprisingly able to take us *Inside Delta Force.*

Reading What You Know

For many years I taught undergraduate courses in literature at various universities, and a point of contention between my students and me arose regularly. Each term, when we reached my lecture on reading aloud, they would argue with my point that the teacher should have intimate knowledge of the text being read aloud. Again and again, I would hear, "But Dr. Layne, it would be more fun if we were discovering what was happening on page seventy-two at the exact same moment as the students. That way we are truly having an experience with them." I would then politely explain to them that if you are discovering what happens on page seventy-two at the exact same moment as your students, you may find yourself "truly having an experience"—with their parents!

I generally have no difficulty seeing both sides of an issue; I'm content to let those who insist Tab is a drink with flavor believe so, and those who claim that all members of the Partridge Family were real musicians may rest easy at night as well. But I cannot support teachers reading a book to kids when those teachers do not have an intimate knowledge of the text. I will not go so far as to call it "bad practice," but I will go so far as to say I do not consider it "best practice."

If you need to get to the airport fast, whom do you want to drive you there: someone who's actually *driven* to the airport before or someone who has been to an airport once in some other city? You can't effectively take somebody to a place you've never been. The richest discussion points, the finest opportunities for skill reinforcement, and the best plot points for visualization are typically more meaningful when prepared for in advance. That's not to say that such a moment cannot "strike you out of the blue," but the majority of the time, you can do the most with a read-aloud when you are the master of the text. You cannot *be* the master of the text when you have no idea where it is headed. In other words, it's hard to follow leaders who aren't quite sure where they're going. (There are *so many comments* that I want to make in this parenthetical expression just now, but instead we're going to play a fun game where you only get to imagine what it is that I am dying to say—and then wonder about it until we discuss it in person.)

There is a scene in Jerry Spinelli's fabulous *Stargirl* (2000) that I capitalize upon for both visualization and writing. It is an emotionally powerful and riveting moment—and I have evidence that it stays with my students long after the book has ended. I say with confidence that there is no way on my initial reading of the book that I could have been ready to make use of that text in the way I do now. In fact, the difference in what I can do with that book when reading it aloud now, and what I would have been capable of doing with it on an initial read is embarrassing. Yes, I would have been "experiencing it" with my students—very authentic—but at what cost?

I will acknowledge the exceptions such as reading aloud a newspaper article on the spot to model thinking aloud for your students or reading aloud from a medical dictionary without preparation so they can witness you struggle. There are always exceptions. Let's not put our energy into creating the arguments; rather, let's acknowledge that the delivery of high-quality instruction *typically* demands preparation on our part. If reading aloud to kids is instruction, then having intimate knowledge of the text (which requires a minimum of one full and thorough reading on your own before reading the text aloud to the students) is nonnegotiable.

FAQs

Dear Steven,

I am writing to tell you about Tanner, an amazing eleventh grader who is smart as a whip, very polite, and always does his homework. It is such a pleasure to have this young man in class in high school English! Of course I don't have favorites, but if I did . . . Anyway the reason for this note is to ask for your advice. I am a strong advocate of read-alouds as I know you are. I read to the kids every day. A few days ago Tanner asked me to read a specific book to the class. His enthusiasm for the book was contagious, and I couldn't let him down, so I said yes. I had not realized that Nicole, who sits near my desk, overheard the conversation with Tanner—and now she has suggested a book she would like me to read to the class. I am not wild about the book she mentioned. What should I do?

A faithful fan,
Bothered in Bemidji

Dear Bothered,

My advice is easy to dispense but hard to activate because I do the dispensing and you do the activating. It will be painful; prepare yourself. Here goes: you need to tell Tanner you made an impulsive decision, and that, upon further reflection, you cannot read his book aloud to the class. If he is as bright and polite as you say, he should understand that opening this door could lead many kids to come forward with their wishes and place you in the awkward position of appearing to have favorites—which, of course, you don't (wink, wink). After you complete your reading of this professional book, I know you will set to work on creating an annual read-aloud plan for the year, so if this issue arises again, you will have added protection—explaining to inquiring minds that you have an extremely purposeful plan put together for your read-alouds and to start adding new titles midyear would throw it all cattywampus and cause you to lose sleep.

At peace,
Steven

I've always been a big advocate for student choice when it comes to reading; how-ever, when it comes to my read-aloud plan—it's *my* plan. Sounds a bit selfish, and it is—but with good reason. As I've already explained, reading aloud to someone or to a group of people is intimate; it's a bonding experience. What happened with Tanner is extremely common. Students become enamored with the sound of a good reader sharing terrific text, and they long to hear their favorite text read by that same reader. But there's a reason you're the adult! You see a bigger picture, and you know that what happened to Tanner and Nicole's teacher would likely happen to you, too. Once word gets out that you'll read student selections, where does that end? How do you choose whose suggested titles will be honored and whose will be discarded?

There's another reason, though, a more important one for avoiding having your read-alouds controlled by a handful of your students. The reason: You are a master teach-er (I hope)! You have an extensive body of knowledge and experience to bring to the table in making these decisions that should go beyond something as simple as "I liked that book."

I want to encourage you to design a read-aloud program with great intentionality, and because we know that reading aloud is instruction, you should expect your program design to be a lot of work! You need to think about what you will read and the time you can actually allocate for reading aloud; it could be very different in every subject and grade level. A key factor in designing a respected and successful read-aloud program will be your rationale for the choices you make. I want you to be able to articulate the gain you are seeking through the use of various texts.

For example, your primary purpose in sharing Sara Holbrook's poem "Naked" from her stirring collection *Chicks Up Front* (1998) could be to attract attention to the genre of poetry and subtly attack any potential negative attitudes. The title alone will cement engagement for sure, but if you read or perform it well, you will be able to hear a pin drop when you are finished. Now you have a chance to begin a discussion about the value of poetry and of powerful language. When you are finished, maybe the attitude meter of the class toward poetry has experienced a tiny, almost imperceptible shift. What happens tomorrow, I wonder, if the bell rings and you say to the ninth graders, "How about another of Holbrook's poems? You up for it?" You may be the only one in the room who knows a poetry unit is coming up in four weeks—you are one slick operator! The gain you are seeking is openness in your students toward a genre that older readers are historically closed to unless they have had a very talented teacher before you came along.

Now that you're a recovering genre-hater, you also want to think about the variety of text types you will share during read-aloud. The wider the range the better, because then you are sending an all-inclusive message to the students that every genre and format has value. Have you ever thought of introducing the graphic novel format via a document camera? Some kids don't know how to read graphic novels—why not teach them! And though you might not choose to read aloud an entire graphic novel that way, you could use read-aloud as an introduction to the format. How about verse novels, newspaper articles, concrete poetry? I don't need to go on; you get the point.

A final point I'll make on this is that I do believe there is some "wiggle room" on the issue of student-suggested read-alouds when it comes to short texts such as picture books, poems, articles, and so forth. It can be very honoring to a student if you choose to share text aloud at his or her request. Short texts can allow for this without completely derailing your read-aloud plan for the year, and they can also be reviewed by you much more quickly than a chapter book could. You simply have to be on guard that it doesn't reach a point where it is out of control—leaving you little or insufficient time to bring forward key texts you selected with great intentionality for this year's class.

Dear Steven,

I'm in trouble and cannot see my way out. I have this group of third-grade boys who hate reading! You say read-aloud helps improve attitude, but not with these boys, and there are a lot of them! I have twelve boys in my room and only four girls! The boys have not been interested in one book I've read aloud this year. Their behavior during my read-aloud time is distracting to all of us. So far this year I have read aloud *The Penderwicks*, *Little House in the Big Woods*, and *The Miraculous Journey of Edward Tulane*, and none of these boys has shown the slightest bit of interest! Today I was right in the middle of my favorite passage from *Because of Winn-Dixie* when Kelso passed gas loud enough to be heard in the next county. He did it on purpose, Dr. Layne, you know he did. What can I do? Maybe my real question is— what would you do?

All good wishes,
Troubled in Telluride

In Defense of Read-Aloud

Dear Troubled,

After reading your note, I am even more troubled than you—I'm sure of it. It may shock you to hear that I am less troubled about Kelso's distribution issues and more concerned about yours—in terms of stories, that is. You have twelve third-grade boys in your room and thus far you have read them four books with girl protagonists— where exciting things happen like stuffed animals are lost, new pets are found, and four daughters go on vacation with their dad. Please get your hands on a book where a third-grade boy is kidnapped or nearly eaten alive—preferably both—as soon as possible, and read it aloud!

Touting some terror,
Steven

The problem Troubled in Telluride is facing is a common one. She would do well to read Teri Lesesne's *Making the Match: The Right Book for the Right Reader at the Right Time* (2003). She has a variety of strong stories in her collection (though I'll pass on *Little House in the Big Woods* [Wilder 1953]), but her placement is completely off track. We don't need research (though it likely exists) to tell us that boys are less willing to read books with girl protagonists than girls are to read stories featuring boys. Any teacher with three years into the profession can tell you that's generally an accurate stereotype.

Twelve boys and four girls—she was doomed from the start with that lineup of books (not to mention we're a little heavy on the realistic fiction genre). Now, you can sell those boys a tear-jerking, coming-of-age tale—you really can . . . but not in the be-ginning. First, you buy their trust by reading heart-stopping, exciting, thrilling stories full of danger, intrigue, and adventure. Then, you slide in a character-driven, soul-stirring tale, and when it's finished . . . LOOK OUT! You better take off like a rocket again—be-cause of those boys! Teachers, there is so much strategy involved in making the best use of read-aloud time. I hope you are seeing that it's not only the selections but the order in which you place them that can determine how much "bang for your buck" you receive.

I know some of you are hoping that I am about to tell you a surefire order in which to line up your selections to ensure you will have the best read-aloud time ever. I can't. It is dependent upon the makeup of your class this year and their needs as a group. No one can tell you what is best, because you are the master teacher, remember? You can scope out a plan over the summer—the way you *think* it's all gonna roll—and I advocate for that. I say, "Yay, you!" if you are putting that time in, but you need to be ready to make adjustments when the kids arrive. It's what professionals do. We prepare, and then we change our plans based on the kids and their needs.

Dear Steven L. Layne,

What does your middle initial stand for? I bet it's Lawrence! I'm right, aren't I? I am really good at guessing middle initials. Okay, on to the important issue. I teach in a wealthy school district, and I have a pet peeve about parents extending our breaks with extra vacation days. These kids go off to their condos in Brussels with their families—and to top it off, they leave three days before break begins, or come back three days late! Obviously, they miss some good chunks of my read-aloud. I say, "Them's the breaks." If they leave early or come back late, they miss a big chunk of the story, but it's not my fault. My colleague Angelica says I should rethink my position on the matter.

Respectfully,

Mad in Morocco

Dear Mad,

I get it. Everyone has a condo in Brussels but you (and me)! From my perspective Angelica is an angel, and I stand with her in asking you to rethink your position. I feel your pain because it is very hard on teachers when parents do this; however, let's also keep in mind that time with our families is precious. It goes by so very quickly, and let's not penalize the kids for the decisions made by their parents. We could go a little easier on the parents sometimes, too—maybe there are those who abuse the break schedule year after year, but most are not chronic offenders. If you know it's going to happen, be kind to your kids and read picture books on those days just before and after break. Who knows, when they grow up, those kids might remember—and invite you to vacation at the family condo in Brussels.

Calling for compassion,

Steven

P.S. Don't quit your day job; my middle initial doesn't stand for Lawrence.

I want to address the calendar for a moment because Mad in Morocco raises an issue many of us face. I alluded to it earlier in the book, but let's give it a bit more attention. What do we do about those long breaks when we have a read-aloud under way? The older I get, the more I strive for simplicity. The simple solution is that if you plan your read-aloud just as you plan all other instruction, you can conclude a lengthier piece of text a few days before a break. Not only can you do it, but if you have reason to believe several kids will be leaving early, you should do it. Likewise, when you return from a break, don't begin a new read-aloud the first day back if that means that some kids will miss the launch. Both before and after the break, at every grade level, it's time for picture books, poetry, articles, and any other shorter pieces of text that will not have consequences for those students who are away from school through no fault of their own. When you stop to think about it, this is a win-win for everyone involved.

∾ Position Statement

This I Believe—About Reading Aloud

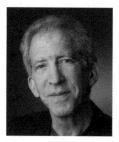

William H. Teale

University of Illinois at Chicago—Illinois, USA
Professor and University Scholar
International Literacy Association Board Member
2011–2014

It was reprised by NPR about a decade ago, but originally Edward R. Murrow's This I Believe *radio show brought to its 1950s audience essays by all sorts of people about the guiding principles by which they lived. I believe that the classroom practice of reading aloud should be a guiding principle for teachers at any level of our educational system. I am convinced that reading aloud is a powerful educative practice: I am convinced by research evidence, and I am convinced by the reactions and subsequent actions of the children and adults to whom I have read aloud over my past forty-five years of classroom teaching. The research (see Van Kleeck, Stahl, and Bauer 2003 for a broad summary) shows benefits for a wide range of student literacy skills.*

The reactions of children and adults to the books as I read to them and the things they do after having experienced a book in this way—reread it on their own, act it out in dramatic play with others, talk about how much they like the author or illustrator, write about their use of the book in a lesson they taught, recommend the book to others, spend their own money to buy the book, and so on—show the effect that reading aloud can have on deep-seated values and emotions. Of course, there are caveats: for reading aloud to achieve its instructional potential, we teachers must think carefully about what, how, and why we read aloud in classrooms. But when we choose a range of high-quality children's, young adult, and adult books; when we read in engaging ways; when we help listeners experience multiple entry points into books; and when we share the joys and depths of literature, we see that reading aloud is indeed a powerful guiding principle of literacy education.

◇ POSITION STATEMENT

Teacher Read-Alouds Nurture Readers

Bernadette Dwyer

St. Patrick's College, Dublin City University—Dublin, Ireland
Professor in Literacy Studies in Education
Reading Association of Ireland President
2005–2006

As a relatively young teacher, I was in the midst of reading Charlotte's Web *(White 1945) to my fourth-grade students. There was not a sound in the classroom; we were all enraptured in the moment, living in the imaginative world of the wise and wonderful Charlotte and her friends. I glanced up from the book, and to my horror, the principal of the school was standing in the doorway of the classroom. He had obviously been there for quite some time.*

My heart stopped, and I hesitated, waiting for a lecture on the importance of meeting standards, fulfilling curriculum requirements, and teaching literacy skills to my students. Instead he paused and said, "Please, don't stop. I was really enjoying listening to you read the story."

Storytelling and indeed story listening is embedded deep into the cultural heritage of Ireland. It is part of our cultural DNA, and we hold literary giants such as Wilde, Yeats, Beckett, Joyce, and Heaney in great esteem. In my opinion, however, people of all ages—from toddlers to grown-ups—love to listen to stories being read aloud. In more than twenty-three years working as an elementary teacher, read-alouds always provided a pleasurable and important part of a balanced literacy framework in my classroom. Indeed, I still engage in reading aloud from a variety of texts and genres with my teacher candidate students at St. Patrick's College. Read-alouds are important for a number of reasons.

First, read-alouds offer pathways into literacy. They provide children with a model of reading fluency. In a sense, children can apprentice themselves to the nuances of reading fluency in terms of rate, accuracy, and prosody when listening to teachers reading aloud. Read-alouds also promote listening comprehension and vocabulary development as children develop their sensory imaginations and their creative and critical thinking capabilities.

Second, teachers who read aloud introduce children to the language of books. Spoken language differs greatly from the literary words in novels and the content-specific vocabulary in informational texts. Therefore, children can be introduced to this language through read-alouds. From my work in high-poverty school districts, both as an educator and as a researcher, I am struck by the paucity of texts in the home. Teachers who read aloud introduce children and teens to a reading culture and help to develop a community of readers in a classroom. In my elementary classroom, children would often choose to leave short texts on my desk and ask that I read them aloud to the class. Inevitably the books I sampled as read-alouds were the first books to be checked out of the class library.

Finally, and most important, read-alouds help to motivate and engage children and foster a lifelong love of reading. Teachers who read aloud allow children to engage and relax in fantasy worlds of witches and goblins, empathize with the plight of courageous heroes and heroines, laugh aloud at and share in the escapades of characters, and learn more about the diverse world in which we live. Teachers who read aloud nurture the readers in their classrooms. Read-alouds help to develop children and teens who can *read, who* do *read, and, crucially, who* love *to read.*

Chapter 4

The Art of Reading Aloud

Dear Mr. Clements,

I believe! That was the resounding thought I heard echoing through my head when reading the last chapter of *Frindle* for the first time. As I turned those final pages, a gnawing thought invaded my brain ... *Look in the dictionary and see if* frindle *is truly a word!* As I looked between the words *frill* and *fringe*, I was disappointed to discover that *frindle* was missing from *Webster's*. However, in that moment, my disappointment became the spark that ignited the passion to make this book a staple read-aloud in my classroom.

I have taught third grade for six years and have read *Frindle* aloud nearly every year. Each time I share this amazing story, it is the same scenario—we get out the *Webster's* dictionary after reading the closing pages and look for the word *frindle*. And each year, as happened with me, a brief look of disappointment crosses the students' faces. They are hoping, as I once did, that you are telling them a true story disguised through the ups and downs of Nick Allen's journey. Their disappointment quickly turns to curiosity (one of a teacher's favorite words), though, which is then followed by reflective discussions about words, courage, risk taking, support, and friendship.

Our discussions have also resulted in some questions about you as a former teacher. A common question that surfaces is whether you have ever had the likes of Nick Allen sitting in your classroom. If so, how did you respond to the Nick Allens you had in class? Were you Mrs. Granger? As a teacher, I think we should all have a little Mrs. Granger in us. I love how she is portrayed as the stereotypical "old school" teacher, yet she possesses a fresh, relevant way of challenging her students, Nick in particular, to push beyond the boundaries of typical school and learns some life lessons along the way.

Thank you, Mr. Clements, not only for writing an inspiring and relatable book for students, but for writing an inspiring and relatable book for teachers as well. This book will remain a staple read-aloud in my classroom because I cannot let go of the curiosity, joy, and revelation it evokes in my learning community. *Frindle* is *excubulant*—my new word for "fabulous" . . . because I say so!

Respectfully,
Theresa Tuttle

Grade Three
Gary D. Wright Elementary School
Hampshire, Illinois

Dear Theresa,

I can't tell you what an honor it is to learn that Frindle *is among your favorite read-alouds. And I find that your kind letter has called up a memory.*

It was the fall of 1971. I was twenty-three years old and greener-than-green, with a shiny new master's degree in my hip pocket—and I had gotten a job teaching fourth grade at a public school in Northfield, Illinois. I taught eighteen boys and twelve girls that unforgettable year. Ability levels were wildly scattered, and, as I was the only male teacher at this grade level, someone had imagined me to be the logical person to deal with the behaviorally challenged. Gratefully, less than a month into this trial by fire, I discovered that reading a good book out loud had an effect on this diverse group that was nothing short of miraculous.

Our first read-aloud that year was The Swiss Family Robinson, *and the response was immediate and astounding. Everyone was quiet, everyone clung to each plot twist, everyone was crestfallen when our read-aloud time ended, and everyone was eager to do whatever it took to be sure the next installment would not be delayed. I was amazed at how deeply they thought about the characters, how clearly they understood the moral dilemmas that came up, and how naturally what we were reading spilled over into the rest of our shared experience. In a week's time there was a fresh sense of classroom unity and mutual respect—which are just two of the wonderful side effects of sharing a good book out loud.*

Regarding Frindle, *yes, I was indeed Mrs. Granger. But I was also Nick Allen and Janet Fisk and just about everyone else, too, all stirred into one big character stew. And when Nick Allen led the kids in taping paper palm trees to the corner of each desk? A boy in that first fourth-grade classroom of mine did that very thing.*

And I think that's the way it works for most fiction writers. I often tell kids that I'm like a miner, and my job is to dig around through my memories and thoughts, looking for sparkling little moments, those bright bits of experience that can be ground and polished and faceted into fictional gems.

After teaching for seven years, and then an additional few years into my work for a children's publishing company, I met Jim Trelease at a bookseller's convention. He was there promoting his first edition of The Read-Aloud Handbook, *and he signed a copy for me. I read it, and the next day stopped back to thank him for so clearly stating the great good that kids and parents and teachers can find as they share literature this way. And many years after that, imagine my delight to find that* Frindle *had been included in a revised edition of his* Handbook. *It was like a great looping story arc had snapped closed to form a full circle.*

Thanks again, Theresa, for your sweet and thoughtful letter—and most of all, thank you for sharing your own love of books and reading with so many children and families.

With very best wishes,
Andrew Clements

In Defense *of* Read-Aloud

I feel sorry for authors and illustrators who aren't good speakers. Why? Because most people expect them to be sensational speakers—just like many of us expect our favorite celebrities or people in positions of leadership to have strong oratory skills. The expectations make no sense, because the skill sets that led to them being published or famous or in charge are quite different from those required of a professional orator, but there remains that expectation among most people.

In a similar way, I believe many of us expect teachers to automatically be skilled at reading aloud. Why? Well, they're teachers, after all—they should automatically be good at it, right? I have had people react with a fair degree of shock and awe when they discover that some teachers express great discomfort with reading aloud. The excuse most often given is "I'm not good at it," and I understand that—completely.

The weight of expectations is heavy indeed, and a teacher who believes himself to be a less skilled oral reader could evade the situation altogether. Avoiding what we feel we don't do well is human nature for all of us, right? So, a teacher who does not engage in read-aloud could be lacking confidence, lacking skill, or simply suffering from the perception that his oral reading skills are not strong enough to "get the job done." I want to open this section by acknowledging three truths with which I hope my readers will agree.

1. Not everyone has a voice and delivery style like James Earl Jones—and that's okay.

2. Avoiding read-alouds because of a lack of confidence in your oral delivery is understandable.

3. The benefits to the kids when we read aloud are so significant that it's worth the effort to do whatever it takes to increase your confidence and/or your skill level. Quitting is not an option.

Those teachers who avoid the read-aloud or greatly limit their use of it because of "performance anxiety" (Stop giggling. You know what I mean! You're just like the kids. Honestly.) have some options if they wish to overcome their issues. The solutions are not complex; they're filled to overflowing with common sense, but often it takes seeing them written down to create the necessary forward momentum.

So, here we go. First, if you think you're not so hot—find out. Do you have someone in your life, a real pal, who will always tell you the truth? I hope so. Assuming that you do, we'll call that person "Pal" with a capital *P*. Such persons can be the game changers for those of us who really want to grow. Go to Pal and set up an observation time—that's with you being the observee (just to clarify). It would be best if Pal can witness you reading aloud to your students. Have Pal take notes and maybe even videotape you. Review the notes, watch the tape together, and listen to what Pal has to say with an open mind. Consider the fact that you might not be the train wreck you thought. This may be all it takes to build your confidence. Yay, you!

On the other hand, let's say this little experiment reveals that you are amazingly intuitive and self-aware (i.e., you're almost as bad as you thought all along). Now, what are you going to do—get a job as a photocopier repairman? NO! You are a teacher—and a very fine one, too. Look at you—reading this professional book! Only true professionals read books to improve their practice. So, you've discovered an area in which some growth is needed—big deal. That took courage, and I can assure you the only teachers who ever become great have to look at their deficits more than once along the road to becoming a true "teacher diva." Ha-ha! What can help you? First—you need to arrange to get into the classrooms of some truly phenomenal performers when it comes to read-aloud. You need to notice everything that's making it work. In particular, pay attention to pace, inflection, enunciation, and volume. Gaining skill in these areas can put you on the high road quickly. You can't do it until you can identify it. That's step one. Bring Pal with you to these sessions if possible. Then, develop a plan to work on one area at a time. You will need to practice reading aloud the exact passages of text you will be reading to the kids—and get feedback before you have your real audience. Sound like a lot of time, work, and commitment? Yep. It's called professional growth. It also happens to be amazingly rewarding. Any of you who go after this, please e-mail me your success stories. I would love to hear them. Keep in mind that working with a professional speech or drama coach (check out your local university) could also be rewarding, and in rare cases it could even be necessary, but I'd suggest trying this more low-key approach first.

Reading with Expression

We all love to listen to someone who can read with expression. Those listening to a story want to be transported into the world of the text. We want to "become one" with the characters or the real-life people we are hearing about; we want to laugh and cry with them; to win and lose with them; and to feel their sorrow, their pain, and their joy. An expressive reader provides that gift to us. We all know what we *mean* when we say "read with expression," but what are the factors that contribute to expressive reading? Chief among them are phrasing and word color.

Phrasing refers to the oral reader's ability to identify groups of words or phrases within a sentence or passage that warrant special attention in some manner and to use his or her voice as a tool to focus listeners on that particular group of words. Isolating specific words for more prominent identification is what is meant by *word color*. Keep in mind that the overall goal of expressive reading is to make the author's message clear to the listening audience. Although that may sound obvious, it is important to note this as the chief objective of expressive reading; if the reader is not clear about the meaning of the text, conveying that meaning through tools such as phrasing and word color can become a significant obstacle.

In Allan Wolf's masterfully written *The Watch That Ends the Night* (2011), twenty-four voices from the *Titanic* recount their fateful story. As readers, we know what is happening in Lifeboat 14 when we hear junior officer Harold Lowe say, "'We've been floating here long enough,' I said. 'I need a few volunteers. We have to go back'" (395). Not only does the oral reader need to *understand* the author's meaning, but *because* the meaning is understood, the phrase *We have to go back* warrants special attention. This is an example of what is meant by the term *phrasing*. In addition, word color is likely to appear when the teacher reading aloud reaches the word *have* in the phrase *We have to go back*. The word has no color of its own, of course, but because we understand the meaning of the phrase (or sentence in this case)—because we have read in the preceding pages about the dissension in that lifeboat over the issue of rowing back into the mass of bodies near the ship—the teacher will "color" the verb *have* to emphasize the officer's determined spirit and resolve to save anyone he can. "We *have* to go back." Likewise, the teacher could choose to color the word *back* or the two-word phrase *go back* and stress both the emotion and the directionality of the moment: "We have to *go back*."

Similarly, in Jane O'Connor and Robin Preiss Glasser's picture book *Fancy Nancy* (2005), a strong oral reader understands from the title, the cover, and the opening illustrations where this story is likely heading. When a teacher prereads the story (which *must* happen), the text and illustrations will indeed confirm that Nancy is a *very* fancy girl. Thus, when the teacher begins reading the story aloud—"My name is Nancy, and I love being fancy"—the second half of the sentence will need special attention (phrasing) and the word *love* will be "colored" to give it needed emphasis.

Now, exactly how does a teacher bring emphasis to specific phrases or "color" specific words? The answer is through a combination of any or all of the following components of speech: enunciation, volume, pace, tone, and pitch. *Enunciation* refers to the clarity with which the sound of speech is created. This includes all aspects of pronunciation and diction, from the crispness of your *t*s to the pureness of your short *a* and every blend, digraph, and diphthong in between. *Volume*, though self-explanatory, deserves to be pointed out, because in the repertoire of a skilled orator, the intentional use of volume greatly shapes the emotional experience of the reader. Failure to alter volume during a read-aloud, particularly when a lengthy passage of text is involved, can be an influential factor in contributing to a "flat" reading that leaves the listener feeling less than inspired. *Pace* is another critical factor. It is paramount for a teacher to be aware of his or her pacing during a read-aloud. Strong use of pace involves adjusting your speed throughout the oral reading to generate excitement, to build tension, or simply to keep the listener engaged. Along with that, a key facet of skilled pacing is the dramatic and intentional use of "pause." Knowing *when* to pause and *where* to pause—and *for how long*—can make all the difference between a solid read-aloud experience and a truly outstanding one. The master teachers, when it comes to read-alouds, are so strong with their pacing that it has become intuitive for them. *Tone* and *pitch* can easily become confused in the minds of those who do not work with oral performance on a regular basis. My colleague Dr. Brenda Buckley-Hughes is a true master of the art of oral performance, and she provides my favorite explanation of the difference between these two terms: *tone* is the quality, the richness (or lack thereof) of the voice during the oration; *pitch* is like the musical note on a scale—it denotes the "highness or lowness" of the sound. When I describe the sound of a voice as "husky," "burdened," "sarcastic," or "light," I am talking about tone. When I become the voice of Baby Bear in the story of "The Three Bears," my tone may be "sweet," but my pitch will be quite high. Make sense? I think you get it.

Some readers are dying for me to talk about people who are monotone readers—right? You kept waiting for it, I know. You were getting worried, but relax. We are there. Central to the issue of those who may be described as monotone readers is one word: *inflection*. Inflection has to do with the modulation (an adjustment or variation) in either tone or pitch, or a combination of the two. It's actually a much less dramatic explanation than some of you were hoping for, but there you have it. Those who are monotone do not inflect; they do not modulate their tone and/or pitch when they read aloud. Generally, this will be true of their day-to-day speech as well. Can it be corrected? Yes. Like most of the facets of my life and yours that we are working at improving, a person can learn to modulate the voice and make use of inflection. Two factors must be present in order for improvement to take place in this area. Factor one is awareness: the person must know that he or she tends to read aloud in a monotone. Factor two is professionalism: the person must desire to grow in this area. What to do if both factors are in play? See my earlier suggestions in this section for those who lack confidence in their oral speaking ability.

Reader's Theater

A prison sentence awaits those who discuss the art of reading aloud without addressing the topic of reader's theater. Although reader's theater does not necessarily involve the teacher in the role of performer, the gains to be made by our students are significant, and reader's theater, like reading aloud, can easily suffer from neglect in a classroom setting. It is easy for reader's theater to be viewed as an "activity," something fun to do once a year, rather than as an instructional strategy with tremendous benefits for kids.

Oral reading by students in the classroom setting is fraught with problems. It has always amazed me that calling on random kids, some of whom are dysfluent, to read aloud in front of the entire class could be viewed as sound practice. If you ask me to do what I don't do well—in front of my peer group—won't that *increase* my anxiety, likely resulting in a more negative performance? And why would you expect to see an appreciable uptick in my fluency by repeatedly putting me in this highly stress-inducing situation? What is more likely to happen is that I will grow up to be a high school student who doodles pictures of teachers hanging from the gallows.

Reader's theater, at its best, allows for a considerable amount of what dysfluent readers need most: practice and preparation. It is certainly possible to toss a script at kids and call on them for an immediate reading performance, but when it is used by professionals who understand why they are doing what they are doing, students will be given time to practice and prepare, not only before the performance, but even before the first official rehearsal. The repetition that takes place through the continual rehearsal of lines not only offers significant opportunity to increase fluency, but also allows the student and teacher the opportunity to address and strengthen other facets of oral reading. Teachers must take advantage of reader's theater to . . . wait for it . . . *teach*! Yes! We can teach the kids about phrasing and word color. We can model how enunciation, volume, pace, tone, and pitch influence delivery. We can talk about and demonstrate for the kids how inflection is needed to avoid a monotone delivery. Moreover, we can stress the importance of understanding the meaning of the text as a first priority (that would be comprehension, which the last time I checked was the actual goal of reading) so that we as oral readers can use our vocal skills to communicate that meaning to a listening audience. My, oh, my, but this sounds a great deal like instruction to me. I've a sneaking suspicion that's because it *is* instruction. So, let's stop thinking of reader's theater as a once-a-year activity and start selecting or writing scripts to keep these kids growing in their comprehension and oral delivery skills all year long.

FAQs

Dear Steven,

My colleague Marguerite likes to have read-aloud time with our combined classes. The kids love it, but I don't. Marguerite does the "voices" of the different characters. I won't do that. I'm just me. There's nothing wrong with just being me, is there? I can't do "voices." Well, maybe I can, I don't really know . . . but I won't. I think the kids will laugh at me. As long as I'm reading aloud, isn't that enough? I don't have to be like Marguerite; she's not as great as everyone says anyway. I want you to tell me that I don't have to do voices like Marguerite, and I'm hoping you will. I'm thinking of telling her that I don't want to do a combined read-aloud anymore and making up some excuse, but you know the real reason: I don't want to do those character voices! The kids might miss being with their friends for the joint read-aloud, I know, but they're kids—they'll get over it.

Your friend,
Voiceless in Victoria

In Defense *of* Read-Aloud

Dear Voiceless,

Bad news. The kids are already laughing at you a great deal of the time; you're just not around when it happens. If you try giving different voices to the characters in your read-alouds and the kids laugh, this time you'll be there for it! Call it an adventure. Providing different voices for characters enriches the listening experience for the kids, so of course they enjoy the read-aloud experience more when that happens. I can't speak personally to the issue you raise of whether there is anything wrong with just being you. There could be plenty wrong if you're insecure, competitive, unwilling to grow in an area of weakness, and not much fun at parties. But I'm sure that's not you. That's someone else.

Giving voice to your issues,
Steven

One of the greatest "losses" for me in leaving full-time public school teaching is no longer having students complain about the substitute teacher when I return from an absence. Early in my career, I learned the wisdom of disallowing the substitute the privilege of continuing my ongoing read-aloud. I would, instead, kindly leave a bevy of picture books from which my subs could choose. And still, the kids would complain. I secretly miss them moaning, "Don't let the sub do read-aloud when you're gone; she does it wrong!" Many of you have had that same blissful experience. It's a real high—until they follow it up by saying something like, "But you could have her back again because other than that, she was the best teacher *ever*!" Leave it to kids to keep us all grounded, right?

Attributing voices to characters is one of the highlights of the read-aloud experience for the proficient oral reader; likewise, it can be one of the most frightening risks to the rookies. How do we actually give "voice" to a character? We're going to head right back to enunciation, volume, pace, tone, and pitch. A character who mumbles (failure to enunciate), speaks fast and low (pace and pitch), and has a frightened, soft style of speaking (tone and volume) is given a "voice" by way of these distinct features. The author sometimes provides us with one or more cues to these different vocal elements in a character's speech; other times, the description of the character's personality is all we have to go on, so our use of phrasing and word color, courtesy of these five elements of speech, are what we must use to convey the personality as accurately as possible to our listeners.

Dear Steven,

Do you remember meeting me at the convention in Pocatello? I was the one in the burgundy poncho with the lime-green Lycra pants wearing a sombrero. Now do you remember me? Boy, Penny Kittle was terrific at that conference. Did you get to hear her? She really got me excited about teaching reading.

Listen, I'm really worked up about Cloris. She says she doesn't see anything in her mind when I am reading aloud. I am good at almost everything I do, but I am particularly good at reading aloud. I'm probably the best I've ever heard. I am thinking of putting myself on YouTube. How can Cloris not visualize, if I am a great reader? I have always had the feeling she does not like me, and I am thinking she could just be doing this to upset me. I have found piles of papers in my room moved around sometimes, and I think Cloris is behind it. This could be like one of those old-time movies where someone tries to make you think you are crazy. If she is doing that, then her claims of trouble visualizing during my read-alouds could all be part of her master plan to throw me off balance. What do you say on the matter?

Thanks,
Crazy in Calabasas

Dear Crazy,

I actually enjoyed writing that greeting more than most. The good news is—at least you're not paranoid. Keep in mind that what you are hearing inside your head when you read aloud could be different from what those listening to you read are hearing. In other words, there is always the frightening possibility that you aren't "all that and a bag of chips" after all, and that Cloris's lack of visualization has to do with your less-than-inspiring delivery. It is equally possible that you are indeed the "phenom" you claim to be, and that Cloris simply needs coaching—small mini-lessons on how to actually visualize. Try inviting kids in class to get up and act out what they see in their minds when you are reading particularly vivid passages that lend themselves to visualization. This will allow Cloris to gain awareness in how many readers "watch the movie" when they are listening to a read-aloud. I don't think she's out to get you, by the way. My gut tells me Cloris is more honest than most, but it's hard to be sure with only my opinion. Why don't you call Penny and see what she thinks?

Sane and stable,

Steven

The term of the day is *visualization*, but when I read aloud to kids, I just ask them (as I suggested to Crazy in that last note and to all of you in Chapter 2), "Are you seeing the movie in your mind?" One of the more interesting facts you'll hear from some aliterate readers is that they don't see anything in their heads when they read silently or when they listen to someone read aloud. I didn't say that's true of all of them, but it is true of many. The skill of visualization has not manifested in these readers, and because it is so necessary and helpful to their development, I want to revisit the issue. The next question is the important one: how do we help them?

First things first—they need to become aware that visualization is a skill put to use by strong readers. How do they learn this is the case? We tell them. We also *show* them. When I am reading aloud a particularly striking visual scene such as the one where Molly Vera Thompson brings her naked Madeleine doll over to Howard's house in *The Kid in the Red Jacket* (Park 1987), I can ask the class, "Okay, gang. Are you seeing the movie in your mind? You know reading is like watching a movie in your head. How many of you have a fairly good picture of the action at this point? Can you see the look on Howard's face? What's his body posture like at this moment? How about Molly's face and body posture?"

By asking these questions of the entire class, I am allowing those who don't visualize to come gently to the understanding that most readers do. Arriving at this understanding can provide some serious motivation for those with a deficit in the area of visualization to try harder. The next step is for me to invite a student to come to the front of the room (with helpers if needed) and literally show us how the scene looks in her mind. Once we've all seen that, I need to say, "Okay. Who saw it differently? Good! Come show us how it looked in *your* mind!" The message from the teacher is clear: it can look different to different people, but most people *are* seeing something. It is has been my experience that following this procedure with a degree of frequency will yield positive results.

I haven't read a lot about the art of reading aloud in the professional literature, which is why I wanted to discuss it with you. I think it's important for us to acknowledge that there is an "art" to performing a read-aloud well. That's why many of you who engage in this process, heart and soul, three times a week or more, are both exhausted and exhilarated when you are finished: it's a performance before a live audience! This chapter is intended to underscore, yet again, that reading aloud is instruction (have you picked up on that theme?).

Consider what we've talked about in these last few pages. First, comprehension is key to effectively bringing the text to life. Second, the voice of the oral reader is a tool that must be used, with intention, to convey the author's perceived message to the listeners. A strong teacher must understand and make use of both phrasing and word color to bring the message forward, and masterful enunciation as well as proficient use of volume, pace, tone, and pitch will clarify the message and allow for the "voicing" of characters. Furthermore, reading aloud is one of the finest methods for reinforcing the skill of visualization or for allowing it to take root. The master teacher, who understands all of this, is able then to transfer these skills to the students through the regular and systematic use of reader's theater.

⤬ Position Statement

Many Reasons for Read-Alouds

Rita Bean

University of Pittsburgh—Pennsylvania, USA
Professor Emerita
International Literacy Association Board of Directors
2002–2006

Reading aloud to my students—both first graders and then third graders—was a daily routine. Both the students and I looked forward to this special time, and there was no way they would let me forget to "turn down the lights, sit in my big chair, and open the book to where we had stopped the previous day." I remember so well their comments when it was time to stop: "Please, please, read a few more pages; don't stop now!"

In Defense *of* Read-Aloud

So, why read-alouds? First, listening to a favorite book proved to be an important means for increasing students' love of and appreciation for reading. I can remember students' eagerness to find out what would happen next to Pippi Longstocking, or what adventure would occur in the novel Island of the Blue Dolphins (O'Dell 1960). This introduction to special texts often prompted them to read the same text on their own—after we had finished the story. Other students would select another book by the same author to read. Reading became something that students were eager to do!

Second, listening to these texts helped students gain an understanding of many difficult words or concepts that they would never have been able to gain on their own. As a colleague of Isabel Beck and Moddy McKeown, I was delighted with their research on read-alouds (2001). The findings of their research about reading challenging texts, those that students could not read on their own, supported the value of read-alouds as a means of increasing students' understanding of world knowledge, increasing their vocabulary, and developing a sense of written language. Yes, the time that I spent reading aloud to students was validated for its contributions to students' literacy and language learning. So, what I had perceived as making "good sense" was now supported by research!

Third, this quiet time, when students had no other responsibility but to relax and listen to a good book was a wonderful way of helping them unwind when they returned from recess or from a particularly active gym class. Sometimes, it was reassuring to them to listen as I read aloud when there were rain- or snowstorms outside and the sky was dark and ominous. Finally (I have to admit it), read-alouds were a source of enjoyment for me as a teacher: a time to enjoy a good book, to chuckle about the humorous events in the story, or to cry when something sad happened. Moreover, read-alouds enabled me to establish a special bond with the students I taught; we laughed or cried together, sharing those moments generated by the content of the book I was reading to them. Reading aloud and watching my students listen attentively, some with heads down, relaxing, and others sitting attentively in their seats, provided important memories for me and were an essential aspect of what I valued about teaching.

I would be remiss if I did not include here a true confession. I remember little about the skill instruction I received in elementary school, but I remember well sitting in a classroom, listening to the teacher read, being disappointed when she stopped, and eagerly waiting for read-aloud time the next day. I attribute some of my love of reading to those early read-aloud experiences, and I thank my teachers for those wonderful memories. I wonder whether some of my former students have similar memories.

❧ POSITION STATEMENT

Anticipation and Shared Enjoyment of Reading Through Read-Alouds

Shelley Stagg Peterson

University of Toronto—Ontario, Canada
Professor, Department of Curriculum, Teaching and
    Learning
International Literacy Association Board of Directors
    2012–2015

Health was my favorite subject when I was in grade four. That's because my teacher read aloud and invited my classmates and me to discuss novels in every health class. She introduced us to the official health curriculum content through the lives of characters such as Beezus and Ramona (Cleary 1955), and Billy and his pet owl, Wol, in Farley Mowat's Owls in the Family *(1961). Alongside the content learning, our recognition of the rewards of reading became stronger with every read-aloud. I can still recall the happy sense of anticipation that I felt when health was on the day's timetable.*

That sense of anticipation is a big part of why I still love to read and constantly seek out ways to carve reading into everyday activity. I believe that for many students, a lifelong love of reading starts with experiences such as the shared enjoyment of stories through read-alouds. Getting into and out of exciting or troubling situations with a character or discovering something new about someone or something somewhere in the world are two of the many reasons that students look forward to read-aloud time and to reading on their own, whether at school or elsewhere. Through read-alouds, students who struggle to read independently or who are learning a new language have the opportunity to enjoy texts that might otherwise not be accessible to them. Their ears are filled with the rhythms of fluent reading, and they are able to share with peers their enjoyment of reading, perhaps by laughing together at a character's outrageous actions, by nudging a friend to take notice of a wondrous piece of information about an animal, or by chiming in with classmates and the teacher on an alliterative phrase that tickles the tongue.

I have come to know read-alouds as "take-students-by-surprise" teaching tools. Even though they do not have the look and sound of traditional instruction (partly because they mirror the reading at home that we encourage parents and other caregivers to do with their children), read-alouds are at least as important as any other instructional tool for teaching reading. Although there may be no deliberate imparting of knowledge or targeted skill development, the list of learning outcomes for read-alouds mirrors language arts curriculum objectives around the world. Enhanced reading and listening comprehension, expanded vocabulary, motivation to engage with texts, deepened understandings about particular topics, and recognition of ways in which language can be used in a range of contexts are among the many outcomes of read-alouds. As teaching tools, read-alouds offer far more to students than what can be described in a specific learning objective.

In today's climate of accountability with requirements that every teaching activity have a specific outcome directly tied to it, I understand that teachers might feel a need to squeeze out read-aloud time for more formal, explicit lessons. Yet there are many reasons (and this book provides an abundance of them) to resist this pressure. Substituting formal reading instruction for read-alouds is like showing a child how to grow flowers by providing a hoe to dig holes but neglecting to provide the seeds or to take the time to watch those seeds grow. There is no doubt that children should be able to use the tools and strategies taught in formal lessons; however, learning how to carry out a particular reading strategy has limited value to students who do not enjoy reading and cannot find reasons to read outside the classroom. Daily read-alouds help students find those reasons, creating an expectation that reading is pleasurable and showing them why they would want to become readers at all.

Chapter 5

The Books We Love to Read Aloud

Dear Mr. Mikaelsen,

As a teacher who advocates and practices read-alouds, I thought I had experienced the best they had to offer. That is, until I selected *Touching Spirit Bear* to read to my sixth graders.

When I first considered *Touching Spirit Bear*, I was attracted to the *survival* genre as well as the inclusion of the Tlingit values. Ultimately, though, I thought of Cole and how many students like Cole I've taught throughout the years. How many students like Cole have been failed by their families? By school? Much like Edwin and Garvey's belief in Circle Justice, I believe in the healing power of books, and consequently selected *Touching Spirit Bear*. At the time, I had no way of knowing just how soon I would learn about the impact of your story.

But first, you must know that the level of student engagement with *Touching Spirit Bear* far exceeds that of any read-aloud I've conducted. Every book has value and students are naturally drawn to oral stories, but I've never been ambushed, blackmailed, or interrupted by my students so they could be assured that our read-aloud would not get stinted. No joke! The kids would actually circle me even before class and barrage me with questions about when I would be reading, how many chapters, whether we could read one extra, etc. I originally planned to end our class periods with the read-aloud, but that proved unsatisfactory for the troops who couldn't risk the thought that our lesson would spill over into our read-aloud time! In fact, during one particular lesson, I was hoodwinked into calling on a student who was waving her hand wildly in the air, the universal sign that she desperately wanted to make a contribution. Imagine my surprise when she instead inquired about when I would be reading *Touching Spirit Bear*. Of course she knew when I would be reading, but the anticipation actually distracted her from focusing on other, less important matters—such as my actual lesson.

From then on, I started our class with *Touching Spirit Bear*, thinking that this would satisfy the students, but that resulted in them pleading for me to continue reading for the remainder of the class. Occasionally, I would entertain them with an extra chapter, resulting in fist punches in the air and hollers of approval. Yet no matter how much I read on any given day, a chorus of groans filled the air when I closed the book. These reverberations actually became customary, contributing to our culture and always making us smile. *Touching Spirit Bear* brought us together as a classroom community every day. In a way, starting our day with *Touching Spirit Bear* paralleled Cole starting his day by soaking in the pond and rolling the ancestor rock; it centered us. Mr. Mikaelsen, why did you choose to represent Tlingit traditions? We often wondered about your connection to this group of people.

Scanning the young faces before me as I read, I saw them connect and empathize with Cole. More important, I saw my students begin to treat one another differently, shifting the atmosphere of our class. Through this shared experience, we began recognizing one another as individuals who each have their own story, and Cole became a fellow student, a friend. Even after we finished the novel, Cole's name continued to pass our lips as if he were on vacation and would be back with us soon. We often pondered what symbols we would carve into our own totem pole, and have the same question for you. What would your symbols be—and what would they represent?

Lastly, I want to leave you with a student's reaction that has resonated with me. Upon closing the book for the final time, students wrote about *Touching Spirit Bear*. One student wrote the following reflection: "Going to school and listening to the novel gave me, personally, a *reason to want to go to school*."

I am confident that reading aloud *Touching Spirit Bear* helped *us* save that student. For that, I'm grateful.

Sincerely,
Stephanie Aspan

Grade Six
Kennedy Junior High School
Naperville, Illinois

Dear Stephanie,

First, I want to thank you for your touching letter. Richard Peck once told me that if I was lucky in my career as a writer, I would have one or two of my novels become larger than me. I asked him when I would know if that happened, and he smiled and remarked, "Well, when they become larger than you." Now, many years later, I know what he meant.

Two of my novels, Touching Spirit Bear *and* Petey, *have both become much bigger than me. Hardly a week goes by that I don't pinch myself, hearing a response like yours. I have had whole states use TSB in their adult penitentiaries where any inmate who reads the novel gets extra hours in the yard. Whole provinces in Canada such as Saskatchewan have purchased readers' sets for every middle grade school in the province. Recognition like this is great for sales, but the responses that really touch my heart are ones like yours. Or when a child writes to me and informs me he has decided not to commit suicide be-*

cause of my book. To know that something I wrote touched a young life, that is what truly makes the long nights and months of writing a novel totally worth the effort. For that, I thank you from the bottom of my heart.

I want to also recognize you, the reading instructor, for your critical role in this process. Without your caring and hands-on use of my book with your students, I would be one hand trying to clap. Only with your efforts in the classroom (in the trenches!) does an author's novel truly come alive. Without your efforts, all of our efforts would be stymied. For that, I also thank you.

I have always tried to write from my heart, providing students with stories and lessons I wish I had been given at that age. I don't want to give them answers, because my answers might be wrong. What I do want to provide to students is a reason to reflect and think. I love independent critical thinking! I want my novel to stay in a child's mind and heart long after she has closed the cover.

To this end, I immerse myself in research before ever beginning the writing process. In Touching Spirit Bear, *I traveled to British Columbia and Alaska, actually jumping into the cold water a mile from shore in late September in my underpants to swim ashore. I tried my hardest to survive but ended up hypothermic in three hours and needed friends to bring blankets and a hot drink ashore from their boat. On that same trip, I had an actual Spirit bear approach within twenty feet of me to pick up a dead salmon lying on the shoreline. I changed and crafted certain parts of* Touching Spirit Bear *because of those experiences, altering my story as needed to be realistic.*

Another aspect that came to bear on this novel was my own childhood being raised in South America, learning to respect indigenous cultures for their wisdom. I did not have a particular affinity to Tlingit culture in TSB but knew I wanted that aspect present in my novel, because banishment has been practiced by First Nation people along the western coast for hundreds of years.

The Tlingit culture happened to be the culture present in the area of Southeast Alaska where I chose to locate my novel.

As for the totem theme in TSB, I have long held a fascination for totem poles and what they represent. I am not a First Nation person with a clan symbol, and as such the personal symbols most meaningful to me and my own life would be the bear and the circle. I would like to always live my life with the quiet inner strength and courage of a bear, and also to know that my life is a part of something much larger, the great Circle of Life where every part of the circle is both a beginning and an end, and everything is one.

The final catalyst for Touching Spirit Bear came when I turned the television on one morning and heard the fateful words, "This morning in Littleton, Colorado, at a high school called Columbine . . ." That was the moment I knew the world needed my book.

Thanks, Stephanie, for helping make Touching Spirit Bear larger than all of us and for helping to make a difference in the lives of young students. They truly are our future.

Warmest thoughts and regards,
Ben Mikaelsen

Welcome to an especially exciting part of the book! Although I've sprinkled a few titles here and there throughout the pages you've read thus far, now we are *really* going to talk books. In her book *A Sense of Wonder* (1995), Newbery Medalist Katherine Paterson writes about our kids, "the best way to cultivate their tastes is to read to them, starting at birth and keeping on and on. 'Let me hear you read it' is a test. 'Let me read it to you' is a gift" (282–283). I hope you'll keep her wise words in mind as you reflect upon all you've read in this book. And now—for *your* gift! You're about to move into a treasure trove of read-alouds from an interesting and highly diverse group of people. Before we begin, I want you to read the next sentence *very carefully. You could easily see a title or an author pop up more than once.* If that happens, instead of getting yourself in a bit of a snit, you must instead say, "Golly gee, that's sure to be a *dandy* book now, isn't it!" (Note: I'm on a mission to bring back the word *dandy*. Please do your part.)

First up, you're going to hear from twenty-six classroom teachers and twelve teacher-librarians from grades K–12. In honor of Junie B. Jones and the very talented Barbara Park, I've asked them to share their "most favoritest read-aloud ever!" The grade level and school identifiers you see here could have changed by the time this book sees print, but all that matters to me is that you know where they were and what they were doing at the time they decided to share these titles with you. And in case any of you wonders later on, the decision to start this section with the classroom teachers and librarians positioned at the head of the line was *intentional*. In other words, I put them right where they belong.

Next up, it's time to hear from the presidents! I've asked nine former presidents of the American Library Association, the International Literacy Association (formerly the International Reading Association), and the National Council of Teachers of English to share their favorite read-alouds with you. I have tremendous respect for those who have led national organizations for literacy; they are knowledgeable and insightful leaders. I am so excited for you to hear about some of their favorite titles.

The line-up continues with current stars. Let's hear about the read-aloud favorites of some of your literacy gurus (and crushes) such as Debbie Diller, Kelly Gallagher, Donalyn Miller, and Frank Serafini! Their stories made me laugh and cry, and I think you'll respond similarly. Besides, it's always fun to gain a little more insight into your heroes.

We'll close up shop with some of my favorite read-alouds of all time. I have to go last because it's my book (and when I don't get a turn, I get really crabby), and because I wanted the opportunity to say good-bye to you for now. Most of all, I wanted to say thank you for spending some time with me, and the best way I knew how was by sharing some of my favorite books.

Books Our Colleagues Love to Read Aloud

You will quickly grab the attention of your kindergarten students with just one word . . . *Stink*! *Stink: The Incredible Shrinking Kid* by Megan McDonald is the first in the series that follows the humorous adventures of James E. Moody, aka Stink. Yes, that is Judy Moody's little brother! This book engaged my students from the very first paragraph. From Stink believing he is physically shrinking, to taking home the class pet, to learning what Presidents' Day means to him, this book—chronicling Stink's adventures—is filled with episodes of sheer fun and delight. My students love that each chapter ends with an entertaining comic strip drawn by Stink. Unleash the potentials of Stink in your classroom and watch joy and laughter fill the air.

Sarah Howe

Kindergarten
Southbury Elementary School
Oswego, Illinois

I love to end the year in kindergarten with my favorite read-aloud, *Junie B. Jones Is a Graduation Girl* by Barbara Park. Although the genre is fiction, the character traits of the boys and girls (not to mention the teacher) in Room 9 are not unlike those found in any real-life classroom. This is what makes these characters so endearing to both my students and myself as a teacher. I love to watch the expressions on my students' faces as they giggle and gasp at just the right moments. The surprise ending gave me goose bumps and melted my students' hearts the first time I read it years ago. I have been reading it ever since!

Patti Rosenquist

Kindergarten
Wild Rose Elementary School
St. Charles, Illinois

I love sharing *Mrs. Piggle Wiggle* by Betty MacDonald with my first graders each year. My students are practically bouncing out of their seats to find out what naughty childhood "affliction" the children in the book need to be cured of next. Excited predictions always abound for how Mrs. Piggle Wiggle will cure the "Never Want to Go to Bedders," the "Slow Eater, Tiny Bite Taker," or the "Fighter-Quarrelers." Reading *Mrs. Piggle Wiggle* has an added bonus because of her old age (copyright 1947). The cultural references and language used are great springboards for broadening background knowledge, building vocabulary, and creating (very!) animated class discussions. First-grade enthusiasm makes it hard to read only one chapter at a time!

Nicole Senn

Grade One
Sycamore Trails Elementary
Bartlett, Illinois

The World According to Humphrey is a favorite read-aloud for first graders. The author, Betty Birney, writes from the perspective of the class hamster, Humphrey, who captures the hearts of my class every year. It is magical to watch my students connect with the book's diverse classroom characters in Room 26. Listening to them mimic me as I read the character of Humphrey aloud demonstrates the power of Birney's writing. The personification used is contagious, and the next thing I know, I see glimpses of Betty Birney's voice within my students' writing. When the book is over, my class begs for me to begin the sequels.

Kristin Erickson

Grade One
Red Oak Elementary School
Shakopee, Minnesota

After listening to more than 230 books, my second-grade students would undoubtedly say that *The Miraculous Journey of Edward Tulane* by Kate DiCamillo was one of their favorites. The rich language expanded our vocabularies, the adventure had us predicting and inferring, and our hearts were touched as we witnessed the selfish hero soften and learn to care about others. My students will remember that it was the book that made their teacher cry, and for many of them, it was the book that proved how carefully crafted words can move them to new emotional depths. We went along with Edward on his miraculous journey, discovering yet again the miraculous wonder of books.

Lori Sabo

Grade Two
Emerald Park Elementary
Kent, Washington

Reading *All About Sam* by Lois Lowry is an excellent way to kick off the year in my second-grade classroom. I definitely have my students' full attention as they eagerly wait for me to read this hilarious book each day. The story is told from Sam's point of view, which really engages my second graders, who love to hear how a baby views the world. It brings me such joy to see my students' smiling faces and hear them laughing out loud as I read about Sam's latest adventure or the mischief that he creates as a toddler. I often hear groans when read-aloud time is over, followed by students' cries of "One more chapter, please!"

Lori Algrim

Grade Two
Wild Rose Elementary School
Saint Charles, Illinois

If you want to captivate your students from the opening sentence and hold them enthralled until the very last page, then take a trip to Giant Country with *The BFG* by Roald Dahl. You'll find fantasy, humor, suspense, and adventure awaiting there; *The BFG* has it all. I've begun every school year for more than a decade with this delightful read-aloud, and it's always a favorite with my third graders. They gasp, shriek, and laugh right out loud at the escapades in this book. The title character's unique way of speaking charms them, and the vivid descriptions and rich language will please any literacy teacher's heart. You can't go wrong with this enduring winner.

Lea Anne Johnson Roach

Grade Three
Sunnydale Elementary School
Streamwood, Illinois

The Lion, the Witch, and the Wardrobe by C. S. Lewis is a classic that stands the test of time. My third graders are simply captivated listening to this fantasy story—eyes wide, begging to hear about the Pevensie children's next adventure beyond the wardrobe. This is the perfect text for modeling the magic of escaping into a good book and engaging our imaginations. My students quickly connect to the characters' eagerness to explore and their sibling squabbles, while deeper discussions arise as my children question Edmund's alliance with the Witch and we examine the theme of good versus evil. Thought-provoking topics and rich vocabulary lead to wonderful learning but don't detract from the pure enjoyment my students experience throughout this story.

Kristen Marchiando

Grade Three
Stuart R. Paddock Elementary
   School
Palatine, Illinois

For three years, *Dodger and Me* by Jordan Sonnenblick has remained a fourth-grade favorite and quickly became the best read-aloud to start my year. I've had tremendous success turning reluctant readers into engaged readers by demonstrating distinctive character voices for Dodger, a blue chimpanzee with orange surfer shorts, and "dumb-old-Lizzie from England." My students keenly listen to the humorous antics of Dodger as he wreaks havoc while helping Willie create a life improvement plan. Not only do my students relate to the characters and themes, but *Dodger and Me* also keeps them hooked until the end—and leaves them wanting more. Fortunately, I can hold up the sequel and smile while my biggest nonreader clamors to be the first to read *Dodger for President*.

Michael Moylan

Grade Four
North Elementary School
Crystal Lake, Illinois

Fourth grade is the year where my students spend time developing their reading identity. In an effort to expose them to various genres and help them find their reading niche, I always make sure to share one of my very favorite read-aloud books with them. *Gregor the Overlander* by Suzanne Collins is an action-packed fantasy that appeals to every student in my classroom. As each chapter ends, my students are begging for me to read more. They cannot wait to find out what will happen next as Gregor attempts to fulfill his destiny in a strange world beneath New York City. With giant talking cockroaches, spiders, and rats as pivotal characters, this book keeps my students engrossed until the very last page.

Jessica Kenney

Grade Four
Fox Ridge Elementary School
St. Charles, Illinois

To start the year in fifth grade, my favorite read-aloud is *Out of My Mind* by Sharon M. Draper. My students immediately befriend Melody, the brilliant eleven-year-old protagonist, who has cerebral palsy, cannot speak, and feels as if she is going to burst from all the words "trapped" in her mind. Resounding cheers and heartfelt tears are my fifth graders' testimony to the power of this realistic fiction novel. I revel in the student-driven discussions and provide several related team-building activities, during which my students get to know themselves and their classmates better. *Out of My Mind* becomes a "favorite fifth-grade read" in my classroom, an honor it consistently maintains all year long!

Heather Kraus

Grade Five
Southbury Elementary School
Oswego, Illinois

The first read-aloud in my classroom is the most important of the year, as it hooks students into read-alouds for the rest of the year and validates me as a consumer of great literature. For me, *The Shadow Club* by Neal Shusterman has been, without a doubt, the best book to accomplish both tasks. By fifth grade, my students can all relate to the main characters' feelings of living in the shadow of another, and the wheels can be seen turning in their heads as they imagine committing the seemingly harmless pranks against their own "unbeatables." However, as the pranks turn from innocent to vicious, students will voluntarily engage in rich discussions of morality, fostering critical thinking skills from day one.

Ben Zulauf

Grade Five
Tioga Elementary School
Bensenville, Illinois

Winter doldrums settle into your classroom? Are you looking out at a bunch of blank, tired stares? *The Schwa Was Here* by Neal Shusterman is the cure! The wittiness of the narrator/main character, Antsy Bonano, will keep students begging for more, and the setting will allow you to have some fun conjuring up your best Brooklyn accent. My sixth-grade students enjoy listening to this comical yet endearing tale about the trials and tribulations of adolescence. The sarcasm and humor lure students year after year, but the real reason I love this read-aloud is the life lessons hidden amongst the pages.

Jamie Diamond

Language Arts, Grade Six
Barrington Middle School—
    Prairie Campus
Barrington, Illinois

While studying the features of science fiction with my sixth graders, I love to read aloud *The Last Book in the Universe* by Rodman Philbrick. Students dive into the post-apocalyptic setting and clamor for more as they transition from loathing the protagonist to rooting for him on his quest. As we delve deeper, my listeners see some similarities between this fictional world and their own through discussions about topics such as instant gratification made possible by technological advances and the effects of increasing gaps between social classes—topics that induce re-markable engagement with these enthralled eleven- and twelve-year-olds. Because of the cliff-hanger chapters, this novel has consistently elicited audible groans and pleas for "one more chapter" four years in a row.

Shane Jensen

Grade Six
Hunting Ridge Elementary School
Palatine, Illinois

I like to start the school year off with a bang and hook my seventh graders right away with a great read-aloud. *Hope Was Here* by Joan Bauer is the perfect title that resonates with my students for many reasons. This novel helps me teach my students what a character-driven book looks and feels like, and how to appreciate it, even if they tend to prefer plot-driven, faster-paced books. There are also many important life lessons embedded within the story, and my students relate to the characters on numerous levels. Our daily discussions, as we explore this title, leave my students wanting more, which sets the stage for the rest of the school year!

Melissa R. Leisner

Language Arts, Grade Seven
Prairie Knolls Middle School
Elgin, Illinois

In Defense *of* Read-Aloud

I love reading Audrey Shafer's *The Mailbox* to my seventh-grade self-contained language arts class. My students are genuinely inspired by Gabe's determination and independence in the face of his emergence from foster care and through the aftermath of his uncle Vernon's death. My students with learning disabilities become confused by books that involve many characters and convoluted plots. *The Mailbox* offers rich development of only a few characters while supplying a simple yet suspenseful and engaging plot. This mystery enticed my reluctant readers and even prompted a few to check it out from the school library. I will continue my annual visit with Uncle Vernon and Gabe through the twists and turns of the "mailbox mystery" for years to come!

Allison Olsen

Language Arts, Grade Seven
Hannah Beardsley Middle School
Crystal Lake, Illinois

Finding a book capable of competing with all the visual stimulation afforded to our children today is challenging. I struck gold two years ago when I discovered *Unwind* by Neal Shusterman. This book is now the first one I read aloud to my eighth graders each year. It is a plot-driven novel that keeps even my most reluctant readers captivated. The students journey with Connor, Risa, and Lev as they attempt to flee the government-sanctioned "unwinding" of unwanted teens. Students find themselves on the edge of their seats at the end of each chapter, begging for more. The storyline facilitates meaningful classroom discussions about contemporary, controversial topics. In addition, tardiness tends to be low because students don't want to miss anything!

Deane M. Gidlund

Language Arts, Grade Eight
Algonquin Middle School
Algonquin, Illinois

Realistic fiction is the perfect genre to start off the school year because it presents a story that students can relate to, thereby sparking their interest. That is why I start the year with *Rules of the Road* by Joan Bauer with my eighth graders. This book generates a lot of discussion with its many real-world conflicts. Strong characters that are well developed and easy to connect to run rampant through the pages of this book! The importance of self-discovery and understanding what family truly means are just a few of the themes that are woven within this novel. Joan Bauer's descriptive, detailed writing style enables my students to go on the journey Jenna takes throughout this novel.

Amy Bender

Language Arts, Grade Eight
Central Middle School
Burlington, Illinois

I love reading aloud *Great Expectations* to my ninth graders! They find themselves inextricably hooked to the mysterious happenings that occur in Charles Dickens's nineteenth-century England. From the creepy convict who literally flips the protagonist Pip's world upside down to the peculiar Miss Havisham and her cobweb-laced wedding cake, the strange characters and intricate plot make for fantastic discussions about Pip's difficulty in reaching his great expectations. My students spend time journaling about their own dreams, connecting to the story's theme about the challenges of reaching one's goals. I find this to be a great book with which to open the school year to implement reader-response assignments that "open up" the kids.

Jerad Beckler

English, Grade Nine
Batavia High School
Batavia, Illinois

As a ninth-grade English teacher, the pressure of finding one book that speaks to all students can be daunting and nerve-racking. Reading *Bruiser* by Neal Shusterman aloud to my students at the start of the year erased such pressure. The fiction novel instantly gripped them. The story of social outcast Brewster Rawlins makes students squirm as many of them can connect with his situation. Other students try to dismiss Brewster as a coldhearted freak, but their thinking is transformed when they realize Brewster's unusual ability to make the sufferings of loved ones vanish—at significant consequence to himself. *Bruiser* inspired my students to deeper levels of empathy and compassion and challenged them to view the "Brewsters" of our world in a different light. Thus, *Bruiser* is my first book choice for next year.

Erica Schwartz

English, Grade Nine
Westminster Christian High School
Elgin, Illinois

In my sophomore American literature class, my students consider the American culture and the intricacies of their heritage. While transitioning to the American dream, I read aloud Thanhha Lai's *Inside Out and Back Again.* Lai's verse novel offers not only a firsthand account of Hà's emigration from Saigon during the Vietnam War, but also a juxtaposition between dated canonical works narrated solely by Americans. Hà's unique account of her struggles to grasp both the American language and culture in limited words keeps my students intrigued as they consider author style through diction and syntax while literally begging for the next passage. This brief but poetic work encourages students to consider different perspectives and experience "America" through another set of eyes.

Andrea Davies

English, Grade Ten
Central High School
Burlington, Illinois

I transferred schools six weeks before the end of the semester. Teaching grade ten classes close to graduation is a difficult task; I needed to connect quickly with my students and create relationships. Reading aloud *The Interrogation of Ashala Wolf* by Ambelin Kwaymullina gave my classes a routine and a way for students to connect with a new teacher. After Ashala is apprehended, she is reluctant to trust anyone but the illegals in the tribe. My students empathized with the challenges facing Ashala, often discussing the choices they might make if they were attached to Chief Administrator Neville Roses's diabolical machine. The fast pace of this dystopian narrative truly captured my students' imaginations. Let the interrogation begin!

Megan Hoult

English, Grade Ten
Montrose Bay High School
Tasmania, Australia

Daring! Adventure! Romance! Sarcasm! What better elements than these to make an engaging read-aloud for eleventh-grade students? If you are looking for a way to get them tuned in, I would recommend you read them William Goldman's *The Princess Bride*. Goldman's tongue-in-cheek tone and extensive use of suspense has my students hanging on my every word, and they practically beg me to read more *Princess Bride* at the beginning of every class. And my response? "As you wish."

Ashley Verhappen

English, Grade Eleven
Wainwright High School
Wainwright, Alberta, Canada

On the first day of each semester, I love reading the introduction to Randy Pausch's *The Last Lecture* to my eleventh-grade advanced composition class. After introducing "the elephant in the room," his terminal cancer, his closing lines of stylistic prose form a thought-provoking essential question: what legacy will you leave? Since I want my students to think of themselves as authors, this versatile text serves as a fabulous exemplar. Reading aloud each brief vignette that composes the major lessons of Pausch's life opens the door to rich discussions on author exigency, audience, and purpose. The premise of "Really Achieving Your Childhood Dreams" captivates my students from the first day to the last, which resonates with their unwritten future.

Thomas Reese Davies

English, Grade Eleven
Central High School
Burlington, Illinois

Senior year can be a challenging, confusing time. The workload of an average Advanced Placement student in my twelfth-grade class is such that time for quiet reflection is often superseded by the demands of colleges, coursework, and extracurricular activities. With this in mind, it came as a breath of fresh air to read aloud David Eagleman's *Sum: Forty Tales from the After Lives*. Reading the vignettes during class led to in-the-moment honest and visceral discussions of the life-and-death issues explored by the text. My seniors enjoyed the connection to the text, and the read-aloud format alleviated the pressure that rigorous readings of complex texts make while heightening the engagement with the ideas and concepts presented in the narrative.

Patrick Escobedo

English, Grade Twelve
Fenton High School
Bensenville, Illinois

I treasure reading *The Alchemist* aloud to my senior English class. This allegory of a man searching for his "Personal Legend" rings passionately in the ears of my young men and women about to venture out on their own journeys. As Santiago peels back the distinct layers of his discoveries, I am moved by the nods of recognition as students piece Paulo Coelho's powerful life lessons into their own, expanding worlds. The exotic backdrop and eclectic cast of characters transport my class to places that they may never visit but now feel that they have. I was apprehensive that a classic novel might fall flat in modern minds. After the first five minutes, that fear was transformed with Egypt's shifting sands.

Kjirsten I. Wilson

English, Grade Twelve
Wainwright High School
Wainwright, Alberta, Canada

During a seventh-grade unit on culture, I read aloud the book *The Legend of the Wandering King* by Laura Gallego Garcia for the students studying Middle Eastern societies. We start the book with soft Persian music playing and a single candle to light the room. My students are enthralled from the first page and run to the library during their break time as well as stay during parts of their lunch to finish the entire book. The gasps of surprises are thrilling to hear as the students realize what the prince will do because of jealousy. The groans when I have to stop reading are equally inspiring. Teenagers begging to be read to—a great collaborative unit!

Barbara Boyer

Middle School Librarian,
  Grades Six–Eight
Shanghai American School–
  Pudong Campus
Shanghai, China

My fourth graders are shocked when I read about the "electrical current war" between Thomas Edison and Nikola Tesla in the book *Electrical Wizard: How Nikola Tesla Lit Up the World* by Elizabeth Rusch. I read aloud this biography to integrate with our students' STEM study on energy. Students are inspired to read Tesla's own belief about the power of children's minds to spark new ideas. The historical references to the first Ferris wheel and the first taste of Juicy Fruit gum connect with them. They are also amazed to learn that Thomas Edison was not a perfect inventor, and they become convinced that more people should know about Nikola Tesla.

Diane R. Chen

School Librarian, Grades Pre-K–4
Hattie Cotton STEM Magnet
   Elementary School
Nashville, Tennessee

My six copies of *How Angel Peterson Got His Name, and Other Outrageous Tales About Extreme Sports* by Gary Paulsen rarely make it back on the shelf after I first meet with sixth graders each year. I show a short *America's Funniest Home Videos* clip of people failing at some sport and then read the first two sections. I never get through the second part before my copies disappear. If there's time, I love to read aloud Chapter 1 —"Angel's Story." Either way, the book travels from hand to hand for most of the school year. The adventures are short, fast, and fun, with relatable characters. It's a great way to generate conversations and build relationships with students!

Jeanie Dawson

Teacher/Librarian, Grades
   Six–Eight
Victory Lakes Intermediate School
League City, Texas

Our school community is made up of expatriates. The student population travels quite a bit and is familiar with living in a foreign community. The ninth graders in the second trimester read and write a memoir for language arts class. To start the unit, I read an excerpt from *Funny in Farsi: A Memoir of Growing Up Iranian in America* by Firoozeh Dumas. Chapter 2's humorous portrayal of Dumas's parents and their approach to mastering English and life in America has components that my students can relate to firsthand. Students enjoy the comical portrayal of communicating in a second language, and it inspires ideas for their own memoirs.

Kathryn Diede

Teacher-Librarian, Grades Six–Nine
Dhahran Middle School–Saudi Aramco
   Schools
Dhahran, Saudi Arabia

When I introduce my eighth-grade students to the Common Core State Standards unit "Looking Back on America," I read aloud *Henry's Freedom Box* by Ellen Levine. This picture book, set in the mid-1800s, speaks to the harsh realities of slavery, which tore children from their families as leaves are torn from a tree, according to Henry's mother. Henry's story shows the strength of the human spirit to overcome insurmountable adversity in a way that my students, who have heard the songs and stories of the Underground Railroad, never see coming.

Jil'Lana Heard

Library Media Specialist,
   Grades Eight–Nine
Lake Hamilton Junior High School
Hot Springs, Arkansas

This one gets a huge smile from my junior primary students. It's hilarious seeing the squeamish looks on their little faces when "Aunty Elsie's" name is mentioned in *Kiss! Kiss! Yuck! Yuck!* by Kyle Mewburn. They relate to having that overbearing relative who pinches their cheeks and constantly tries to slap on some sloppy kisses. They always feel the need to share funny stories about where they've hidden to avoid "their" Aunty Elsie. It's humbling, seeing expressions change toward the end, when Aunty Elsie is injured and can't visit for a while. Like Andy, they realize that they, too, will miss the attention. It's an exciting Monday read-aloud, with all children often reading the fun repetitive bits aloud with me.

Shahieda Khan

Primary School Librarian,
    Years One–Six
Rosebank School
Avondale, Auckland, New Zealand

Close your eyes . . . envision your library . . . students sitting around a makeshift campfire complete with flickering flames, and your only light is a flashlight to read stories from *Scary Stories to Tell in the Dark* by Alvin Schwartz. To kick off the seventh-grade unit on writing scary stories, I read selected stories to illustrate suspense, characters, and settings that are needed for the horror genre. The atmosphere and readings captivate my students and climax as the last story ends in a horrifying scream. With adrenaline pumping, students begin discussing the elements needed to write their own stories. Weeks later, having completed their own writing, my students are sitting around the campfire again—hoping, this time, to scare one another (and me) with their stories!

Laurel Marion

Middle School Library/Media
    Specialist, Grades Six–Eight
Jackson Middle School
Jackson, Ohio

I am reading to grade one students, and they are leaning forward. They are imagining themselves as Brian, the little boy in *The Salamander Room* by Anne Mazer, who takes a salamander home. Mother asks Brian, "Where will the salamander live?" In Brian's bedroom, of course! For every roadblock Mother presents, Brian has a solution. The rain forest that Brian visually develops in his bedroom is a delight, and you can see the students imagining the room: one with open sky, birds, insects, and trees abounding. Capture the imagination of these young minds as they are drawn into the world of . . . what next?

Linda Scharbach

Teacher-Librarian, Grades K–5
Aspen Grove Elementary School
Grande Prairie, Alberta, Canada

During the Indiana High School Basketball Tournament, I read aloud to my ninth graders from the picture book *Hoop Genius: How a Desperate Teacher and a Rowdy Gym Class Invented Basketball* by John Coy. Indiana is a basketball state, and this book is an instant hit! My students are surprised to find that basketball was not created *in* Indiana, and Coy's narrative, which can be read in about five minutes, makes them think about the history behind the sport. I love sharing the great author's note at the end, too!

Gigi Shook

High School Media Specialist,
   Grades Nine–Twelve
Center Grove High School
Greenwood, Indiana

I love reading the narrative *The Fiery Salamander* by Australian author Colin Thiele to my preps and grade one children! It usually takes two readings, and I stop at the halfway mark, which leaves them up in the air and wanting more. I get the children to predict what will happen to the fiery salamander and if the animals will be able to "finish him off," so to speak. Their little faces light up as they all want to have a go at saying what they think will happen. I make sure that I read it with lots of expression, too!

Deb Smith

Teacher-Librarian, Grades K–6
Lansdowne Crescent Primary
  School/ Illawarra Primary
  School
Hobart, Tasmania, Australia

Our high school organizes a reading program called One Book, One School in collaboration with the school library and the English department each year. In preparing our students to read *The Hunger Games* by Suzanne Collins during the summer break, we read an excerpt in their English classes and to incoming freshmen at their middle schools. Since I read to more than 200 students at a time, it is imperative to read aloud a passage that will keep my students engaged. By selecting and reading the last fourteen paragraphs of the first chapter, but leaving out the last sentence and closing the book, the silence anticipating the name that was chosen as the tribute for District 12 is deafening!

Debbie Turner

Library Media Center Director,
  Grades Nine–Twelve
Metea Valley High School
Aurora, Illinois

Koala Lou by Mem Fox never fails to engage my students in K–2; they hang on every word. Lounging on our soft, inviting cushions, the children are lulled into storyland by the wonderful rhythm of the cuddly, warm fuzzy feeling you get from a great story being read aloud. This picture book, full of cute Australian animals, draws the children in closer and closer as the story develops and allows me to go wild with the characters' voices. Our four copies of this book are never on the shelf after I have read this story!

Jo-Anne Urquhart

Teacher-Librarian—Early
  Learning Centre, Grades K–2
St. Stephen's School
Perth, Western Australia

Books the Presidents Love to Read Aloud

From Presidents of . . .

The American Library Association

I learned to read at a very early age and was taught that the ability to read was a powerful skill. Learning to read allowed me to acquire information as well as to gain understanding in deciphering meaning. After I had learned to read, my parents had me read to them; however, it was not until I was an intermediate reader that I understood reading aloud and that giving a voice to what was being read was as powerful as the ability to read itself. The idea that I could unlock the same magic of being read to by reading aloud myself really blew my mind!

My favorite read-aloud is Nikki Giovanni's poem "Ego-Tripping (there may be a reason why)." I have read it as a student in front of my peers in a women's studies course and as an instructor for a course cross-listed in African American studies.

Reading the poem silently is enjoyable, but when it is read aloud, it comes alive. The quality of the writing provides rich and vibrant imagery that can be appreciated by black and white, young and old, men and women. "Ego-Tripping" invites me to explore Ms. Giovanni's voice with my voice—*as* my voice. As I near the end of my reading, I become as she describes:

> *I am so perfect so divine so ethereal so surreal*
>
> *I cannot be comprehended except by my permission.* (1973, 5)

Reading aloud is a celebration of the power of reading that can never be taken away from me.

Courtney L. Young

Librarian and Professor of
   Women's Studies—
   Pennsylvania State University
American Library Association
   President 2014–2015

I cannot remember a time when I did not read. Growing up, I read for the pure pleasure of getting to know interesting people, dipping into their lives, and imagining myself with their characteristics. As I got older, I started reading about human experiences that troubled me—the Holocaust, racial discrimination, and war. I consumed these books; they helped form the development of my soul.

When I became a teacher and school librarian, I discovered many students who had never experienced reading as pleasure or inspiration. I found that I could break through their barriers by reading books to them aloud—if I picked just the right books. One such book is *Show Way*, written by Jacqueline Woodson and illustrated by Hudson Talbott. In lyrical text and exquisite illustrations, Woodson and Talbott have captured the multigenerational experience of the women in Woodson's family, from slavery to the future possibilities for Woodson's own daughter.

Why do I love to read this book out loud to young people? From the opening page, when Soonie's great-grandma is sold away from her parents at the age of seven with only "some muslin her ma had given her," two needles and thread, the students are totally engaged. They listen to the stories of Big Mama and realize that "all the stuff that happened before you were born is your own kind of Show Way." By reading the book together, we can share our reflections on the human side of history and help each other envision roads to the future.

Barbara Stripling

Assistant Professor—Syracuse
University
American Library Association
President 2013–2014

I live in Alaska, where the winters are dark and harsh, the spring is short, and the library has big windows to let in ambient light. Arctic lupine blooms in May before school is out. It's a time when high school seniors are ready to begin new lives and head near and far for school, work, the military, or to just take a year off to think about what might come next in life.

For me it is always a time to think about the gift that I want to give as part of "senior send-off." Reading aloud to high school students—one might think it a daunting task: won't they be bored? But like adults, their childhood is inside of them, and everyone loves a great story well told. I choose *Miss Rumphius*, written and illustrated by Barbara Cooney, as a wonderful read-aloud for them. It has a message particularly apt for those beginning a new life: see faraway places, live by the sea, and do something to make the world more beautiful.

It's easy to sit on the floor with young children gathered around—not so easy for high school, so I put the pictures into a simple PowerPoint they can all see. I read and ask the students to pin pictures from the web (with Pinterest) of faraway places they want to see and places they might live by the sea. It is difficult at eighteen to know or even imagine how you can make the world a better place. They make suggestions, many of them brilliant and touching, as lovely as the purple flowers sowed by the Lupine Lady in the children's book *Miss Rumphius*. We just make the world a more beautiful place.

Ann K. Symons

School Librarian—Retired—
 Juneau School District, Alaska
American Library Association
 President 1998–1999

The International Literacy Association

Choosing one favorite read-aloud is quite a challenge. I love reading aloud, and have witnessed its many benefits not only in K–12 classrooms but in my university courses as well. I especially appreciate the power of the read-aloud in content-area classes such as science, mathematics, and social studies; but all of that said, I have concluded that my all-time favorite read-aloud is a book I read to my nephew Connor's kindergarten class last year. It is titled *Giraffes Can't Dance*. It was written by Giles Andreae and illustrated by Guy Parker-Rees.

Giraffes Can't Dance is a story about Gerald the Giraffe's inability to dance, which becomes quite evident at the Jungle Dance. The warthogs waltz, the lions tango, the chimps cha-cha, and the baboons engage in a Scottish reel, but Gerald can't dance. I mean it. He really cannot dance. He tries, but the outcome is very embarrassing. Feeling very alone and inept, Gerald slinks away from the dance. Then, when he is all alone, he starts to sway to the sounds of the night. As he continues listening to the music, he starts to shuffle, leap, and somersault. At last, he cries, "I am dancing!" Of course, all the other animals have gathered around to witness Gerald's fancy steps and conclude that, indeed, giraffes can dance!

For me, this story is about the special gifts each of us possesses. I love hearing affirmations of this when I read it to the children. As Olivia, a student in Connor's kindergarten class observed, "We all have special gifts, and that is a great and wonderful thing."

Maureen McLaughlin

Professor—East Stroudsburg
University of Pennsylvania
International Literacy
Association President 2013–2014

As a child I was fascinated by history and historical fiction. I'm not sure why, but I spent hours at my desk in the one-room country school I attended through sixth grade just reading books with a historical emphasis. In college, I was an American history major because I thought I was going to become a high school history teacher and football coach. In the end, I became a fourth-grade teacher and then a reading specialist. In both of those roles, and as a father as well, I became the purveyor of historical texts. I read and recommended such texts to my students and my children.

One book, *The Matchlock Gun* by Walter Edmonds, began this journey into historical texts. It was my "home run" book! I think I was a third grader when I first read that book, and it captured my imagination. Briefly, it is a heroic story set in the era of the French and Indian War in a setting near Albany, New York, where I ultimately worked for a quarter century of my professional life.

I have read that book to many fourth-grade students. I try to set the historical stage and have them imagine living in the wilderness with not a neighbor in sight. I even point out the Eurocentric point of view the author takes and ask students to consider how the story would be different if a member of the Iroquois nation had written it. But *The Matchlock Gun* is only one of the many examples of historical fiction I've read aloud.

I'll close by noting *Turn Homeward, Hannalee* by Patricia Beatty—another historical text that I've read aloud frequently. This book is set in the era of the Civil War and features a working-class girl as the heroine. As is the case with *The Matchlock Gun,* this book invites readers to imagine life as a child during a historical era that is very different from today. I've always assumed that such books can bring history to life and make readers consider just how different children's lives were then compared with their lives today.

Richard Allington

Professor—University of
    Tennessee
International Literacy
    Association President 2005–2006

As a volunteer in the St. Louis Public Schools with Reading Is Fundamental, one of my roles is reading aloud. My selection, *More Than Anything Else,* is a tribute to dreaming, authored by Marie Bradby. Her descriptive language provides visions of the story's setting, the toil of the father and two sons as they labor from sunup to sundown, and the pain felt in their bodies at day's end.

One son, Booker, has a stomach rumble for food, but a deeper hunger to learn to read. When it is revealed that Booker is nine and unable to read, I see questions in the students' eyes. Inevitably one child will ask, "Why can't he read?" Continuing with Booker's story, I read about him seeing a man reading a newspaper aloud to others gathered around. Booker's excitement at the thought of being able to "learn this magic" has his heart racing. His mother senses his yearning and surprises him with an alphabet book, and now he adds writing to his dreams.

As Booker copies the book's alphabet marks on his home's dirt floor, I have students join me as we make our marks in the air. The students' anticipation grows until Booker again meets the newspaper man, who agrees to teach the boy to read and write his own name. Imagine the students' surprise and joy when I read that the boy's name is Booker T. Washington and his dream, something he wanted more than anything else, has finally been fulfilled.

Dolores B. Malcolm

Administrator—Retired—
   St. Louis Public Schools, Missouri
International Literacy
   Association President 1995–1996

The National Council of Teachers of English

"That's the end?" The kids look at me in astonishment. I close the book and nod. Their voices explode into the silence, arguing and speculating about what will happen to a character whose fate has been left uncertain.

For many years, the books that I selected to read aloud left both my audience and me sighing with warm satisfaction as the story neatly came to completion. Then I started reading international literature and realized that the requisite happy ending was *not* universal. The need to have everything brought to closure, with the loose ends neatly tied together, was a trait of American children's books.

As I read aloud books from other parts of the world, I came to value books that left me feeling uneasy or even disturbed. An open ending invites dialogue because listeners feel an intense need to talk with one another. One of my favorite read-alouds is *Fox* (Wild 2006), about Fox, who persuades Magpie to leave her friend Dog, only to abandon her far away in the hot desert. As Magpie huddles in despair, unable to fly in the burning heat, she remembers Dog and takes a tentative step toward home. The book ends with that step—a step of hope but not a step of certainty.

This difference between an ending of hope and a happy ending signals a respect for the minds and imaginations of readers. Readers are invited not to sigh happily at how the author has resolved the conflict but to bring themselves into that story world and conflict. They are invited to take a stance of inquiry and complexity, instead of receiving easy answers.

Kathy G. Short

Professor—Language, Reading and
Culture—University of Arizona
National Council of Teachers
of English President 2015

One of the most critical tasks we do for children is encourage their delight in the beautiful melody of language. Receiving the printed word, as one linguist phrased it, "as a flow of speech sound through time," can induce wonder. Amidst all the concern for testing comprehension of individual words and their combined meanings, we can lose sight of the magic of words, whether somber, serious, or silly.

One of my favorites can delight kindergarten children through college students. Read Lewis Carroll's "Jabberwocky" aloud and do it more than once. "'Twas brillig and the slithy toves did gye and gimble in the wabe..." Any group will include some individuals whose imagination is set alight by those rollicking words. Others at any age are so bound up in language as only a conveyance for literal meaning that they won't enjoy the poem the first time. Persevere subtly to open possibilities.

When I first experienced the poem unaccompanied by illustrations, the words intrigued me. Since then, many artists have been inspired to cast the language into visual images. Recently I've been using the illustrations by Stephane Jorisch (2004) because they represent the word *fantasy* in surreal images. Not as easy to appreciate as more realistic art but worth studying to discover the appeal.

Talk with children about the words. Which do they remember, which held their favorite sounds, which could they use in a made-up sentence of their own? This can open up the question, Why did the poet choose to make up words? Examining words for their personalities can lead to an intrinsic curiosity and appreciation of the power of language that will be useful and a lifelong pleasure.

John Warren Stewig

Professor of Education—Retired
—Carthage College
National Council of Teachers
of English President 1982

"[T]he secret of wisdom is to be curious—to take the time to look closely, to use all your senses to see and touch and taste and smell and hear. To keep on wandering and wondering." These sentences, my favorites from Eve Merriam's *The Wise Woman and Her Secret* (1991), are a response to Jenny, the curious child who asks why she alone was able to discover the wise woman's secret. I slow down to highlight the poetic rhythm of the phrases. For me, a progressive educator, this story reflects the essence of learning and the height of good teaching. I want my listening audience to learn from various perspectives and contexts. So when I speak to audiences of researchers, professors, parents, and teachers, I often select and read aloud illustrated books written for children and adolescents that relate to the message of my presentation. Whether I talk about the reading process, human rights, language development, young children, or reading evaluation, I try to show connections between the scientific aspects of my talk and the humanistic aspects of life experiences expressed in literature for children and adolescents. I hope to engage them in attending to the diversity of learning and teaching possibilities that I refer to in the academic aspects of my talk. Authors who write for the young are also teachers—engaging readers' imaginations to "find more to marvel at in this curving, curling world that spins around and around amid the stars."

Yetta Goodman

Regents Professor Emerita—
 University of Arizona
National Council of Teachers of
 English President 1979

Books the Literacy Stars Love to Read Aloud

I love reading aloud—literature, informational text, *and* poetry! I've read aloud to children everywhere . . . on carpets and under trees at school, in libraries, on bunches of pillows at home, on the phone to my friends, and even in the car on family trips. We make time for what we value, and I value reading aloud!

My favorite read aloud? It's impossible to choose just one. Lately, it's the Scaredy Squirrel series by Melanie Watt, a French-Canadian author. (Share more about her with your kids via videos on www.TeachingBooks.net.) I'm always in search of new books (and authors) for teachers to share in their classrooms, so I was delighted to find these on a trip to Toronto.

I love a strong character, and Scaredy Squirrel does not disappoint! His neurotic behavior and extreme need for order appeals to my sense of helping teachers (and their students) feel calm in the midst of the sometimes-storm of everyday teaching and life. Melanie Watt's creative illustrations make me smile; so does her extensive use of labels, lists, and schedules. Her books are quirky, delightful, and have a strong message. Scaredy Squirrel takes a risk and jumps into the unknown. May you and your students do the same. You're guaranteed a safe landing and lots of laughs in the capable hands of *Scaredy Squirrel . . . at the Beach . . . Makes a Friend . . . at Night . . . Goes Camping*, and more!

—Debbie Diller

I particularly enjoy reading aloud texts that defy grade-level classification. My current favorite is *The Day the Crayons Quit* (Daywalt 2013). Each crayon has a complaint for its owner Duncan. Orange and yellow, for example, each believe that they are the better illustrator of the sun, and provide evidence for their claims. Pink crayon complains about gender stereotyping. Gray crayon complains that he has to work too much, and it isn't fair. The text allows readers to explore equity and invites them to consider how Duncan responds to their complaints. For older students, it invites an analysis of various forms of argumentation.

Although equity for crayons is my current favorite, my all-time favorite is *The Children's Story* (Clavell 1963). My fourth-grade teacher read this book aloud to us as we sat under our desks. The Cold War was the talk of the day, and my teacher wanted us to understand the impact of being conquered by others. What we missed, at that age, was the influence that teachers have on students' understanding of the world. If you haven't had a chance to read this book, do so immediately. I've read this book aloud every year that I have been a teacher to K–12 students and to future teachers. We are powerful when we share words and ideas with our students, and it doesn't hurt to be reminded to use that power wisely.

—Doug Fisher

IN DEFENSE *of* READ-ALOUD

Thirty years ago, as a student teacher, I nervously read a chapter of *Lord of the Flies* aloud to a room full of rambunctious sophomores. I was scared to death and it must have shown, because the next day I walked into class to find a paper cutout stick figure of me taped to my podium. It was labeled "Mr. Mono" (as in *monotone!*). Ouch.

I have come a long way since then. To say I read aloud to my students today would be an understatement—it would be more accurate to describe my readings as performances. Whether I am singing "Beasts of England" in *Animal Farm* or orating Hamlet's "To Be or Not to Be" soliloquy, I am now the opposite of Mr. Mono—I lean into the readings.

My favorite read-aloud remains Atticus's closing argument in *To Kill a Mockingbird*. It starts with a double entendre—"This case is as simple as black and white"—and rolls into a passionate plea to spare Tom Robinson's life. Take the following excerpt:

> *But there is one way in this country in which all men are created equal—there is one human institution that makes a pauper the equal of a Rockefeller, the stupid man the equal of an Einstein, and the ignorant man the equal of any college president. That institution, gentlemen, is a court.* (Lee 1960, 205)

Doesn't this passage invite itself to be read aloud? The entire scene, which takes fifteen minutes to read, begs to be read with passion, with verve, with conviction. To read it any other way would be unjust.

I can't wait until I get to read it again.

—*Kelly Gallagher*

Reading aloud to primary-age learners has always been a delight, but I must plead guilty to spending too many years focusing on fiction-based read-alouds. I was afraid that informational selections couldn't possibly hold the attention of my ever-so-wiggly five- and six-year-old students. But how wrong I was! Once I began to experiment with read-alouds from the masters of nonfiction such as Seymour Simon, Nicola Davies, Gail Gibbons, Melvin Berger, Doreen Rappaport, and so many more, my students erupted with questions and ignited a sense of wonder that electrified our learning.

Although I have come to treasure many nonfiction authors, I must admit that Steve Jenkins's *Actual Size* holds a special place in my heart. On the very first page, Jenkins hooks his readers with an invitation to join him in comparing themselves with the actual size of the creatures in the book. From that moment forward, I delight in watching as children's eyes go wide and they gasp in amazement over massive foldouts that reveal the actual size of a crocodile's head or the enormously long legs of a Goliath frog. When you open the page with the hand of a gorilla—actual size—children can't possibly resist placing their hands directly on the page to compare the image with their own small fingers.

This is a book that is guaranteed to wear out quickly, because primary children enjoy it so much, they want to read it again and again and again. What a beautiful way to enter the magical world of informational literacy.

—*Linda Hoyt*

I was a good girl in school. My mother, great-aunt, and grandmother were teachers and never missed an opportunity to remind me that teaching is a hard job and that I needed to behave and thank my teacher every day. In second grade, my teacher, Miss Shakelford (she was exactly as you imagine), read *Pippi Longstocking* aloud to us, and it dawned on me for the very first time that being naughty could be fun. Pippi ran positively wild and got away with it. Pippi didn't need her father; no one told her what to do. I resolved to be naughty and to wear my hair in uneven ponytails. My first bold act was to *pretend* to chew gum while Miss Shakelford was teaching. I chomped on my imaginary gum with great vigor, longing to be caught and scolded. Pippi would have had the perfect comeback, and I was certain I would, too. I never got caught—one of the great disappointments of my K–12 educational experience!

When I taught second grade, I read *Pippi Longstocking* aloud to my class and waited for the naughtiness to begin. Sure enough, I had a gang of little Pippis, and they were far more clever than I had ever been—no imaginary gum chewing for them! Gilbert decided to make a break for it during recess and was found a couple of hours later in a downpour, making his way home. Lacey and her accomplices made alterations to a couple of class photographs—with permanent ink. And they didn't just draw mustaches. No, they added "talk bubbles" and supplied some juicy quotes from the subject of the photo. Secretly, I loved those feisty kids. I had to suppress a smile or a giggle more times than I can count, and I thank Pippi for reminding us that being a little bit feisty is more than a little bit good for us. Feisty has served me well as an adult, though the ponytails are probably best left in my naughty past.

—*Ellin Oliver Keene*

It's no secret that high school students can be hard to captivate. It's no secret that many have stopped reading by the time they enter their teenage years. Each day my mission to re-create readers begins with read-aloud. It is the single best way I know to call my students to literature, nonfiction, and memoir.

"Listen to this voice," I tell my students, "and you will hear David Finkel speaking just to you. He begins *The Good Soldiers* [2009] with this passage: 'His soldiers weren't yet calling him the Lost Kauz behind his back, not when this began. The soldiers of his who would be injured were still perfectly healthy, and the soldiers of his who would die were still perfectly alive' [1]. This writer has a story from Iraq that will change what you now think about war."

The next day I begin again. "Last winter I heard Marina Nemat speak about the years she spent in an Iranian prison. Imagine—just sixteen years old when she was captured, tortured, and sentenced to death because she would not reveal the names of her friends. Her memoir, *Prisoner of Tehran* [2008], tells you of her life before, during, and after captivity in beautiful detail. Here's a glimpse: 'As a young child, I loved the sleepy silence and dreamy colors of Tehran's early mornings: they made me feel light and free, almost invisible. This was the only time of day when I could wander inside my mother's beauty salon; I could walk between the styling chairs and hair dryers without making her angry' [21]."

Day after day, I call my students to the lives lived between the pages of books. I surround them with the irresistible pull of words to name what is in our hearts and what is in our lives.

—*Penny Kittle*

In Defense of Read-Aloud

My audience for read-alouds is a little different now that I teach graduate library science students in a fully online program. However, the book I read aloud has not changed in the twenty-five years I have taught children's literature. *Everybody Needs a Rock* with words by Byrd Baylor and illustrations by Peter Parnall (1974) remains the first book I share with students in my class (though now I do it in video format).

I love the sparse use of earth tones in the illustrations and the incredibly rich language of the author. It is a story of a girl sitting in the desert talking about finding special rocks that you find by yourself and keep forever. There are rules, of course, for finding those special rocks—ten rules!

Why has this book continued to be a "go-to" for me all these years? Simply, the rock for me is the perfect children's book. I talk about how the students will read many books during the semester (they read about 100 books). I tell students that these books might not all be special books from their perspective. However, I do encourage them to talk about their own "rocks," those books they found on their own and share with their own classes over and over again. *Everybody* needs a rock!

—*Teri Lesesne*

My favorite book to share and read aloud with my upper elementary students every year is Rebecca Stead's magical book *When You Reach Me.* The book appears to be a simple story as readers follow sixth-grade Miranda through her daily life in the late 1970s—going to school; reading and rereading her favorite book, *A Wrinkle in Time*; walking past homeless people in her New York City neighborhood; and coaching her mom, who's trying to earn a spot on *$20,000 Pyramid.*

Stead weaves a brilliant puzzle as the connections between seemingly random events emerge—Miranda's best friend Sal gets in a fight with a new kid, items disappear from Miranda's apartment, and a string of mysterious notes appears, each one more urgent and frightening. My students are drawn into the story—racing to solve clues before Miranda. I set aside most of a class period to finish the final two chapters, because my students are on the edge of their seats during the book's climax.

When You Reach Me challenges my students because they lack historical context for the 1970s—yes, it's *history* to them. We watch old episodes of the *$20,000 Pyramid* (thank you, YouTube!) and talk about latchkey kids—a term my students don't know. The pace of the book is slow but deliberate. It takes time to fall into the narrative, and the random nature of the plot requires attention to detail. As the final pieces fall into place, students express wonder at how cleverly each part fits into the larger mystery. Many students choose to reread the book, looking for evidence of future events in tiny moments. Students see the foreshadowing on a second read—and they're delighted by it.

—*Donalyn Miller*

"The night Max wore his wolf suit and made mischief of one kind and another..." The opening lines of *Where the Wild Things Are* sets the tone for its own reading. To say that I read aloud this book would diminish the emotional and embodied nature of performing a picture book like this. You have to roar your terrible roars, gnash your terrible teeth, and roll your terrible eyes to bring this story to life. It doesn't matter if it is preschool or graduate school. You gotta be the book!

To say I connect to the character is an understatement. Max is deeply embedded in my memory, and probably my psyche as well. There are times in my life when I *am* Max. I have sailed away in a red boat and longed to be where someone loved me best of all—just another rebellious boy with an inexhaustible imagination, making mischief of one kind and another. Who thought you could make a career out of that? And my own actions have usually ended with similar results: being sent to my room, office, classroom, or doghouse without supper.

Each time I read this picture book, I revel in Sendak's language as his words spill across pages, slowed down only by my desire to linger a bit longer in the illustrations. When Max returns home exhausted, I am as well. I close the back cover, satiated, but comforted in knowing I can return again and again to *Where the Wild Things Are*.

—*Frank Serafini*

I wish I could say I have one treasured chapter book that I've read aloud to my first graders year after year. It seems that the book I love changes with each new group of learners. Once I get to know my students' interests and the personality of the class, I select read-alouds that will challenge their thinking, spark ongoing conversations, and motivate them to read, read, read.

So, when I first started teaching (almost three decades ago!), we mulled over themes of friendship, big dreams, and overcoming fears by discussing classics I would read aloud such as *Charlotte's Web*, *Mr. Popper's Penguins*, and *James and the Giant Peach*. Since its debut in 2007, I've read them Brian Selznick's captivating book *The Invention of Hugo Cabret*, and we've spent hours pondering the words and illustrations.

Recently, a kindergarten teacher and fellow read-aloud enthusiast handed me *Lulu and the Brontosaurus* by Judith Viorst. For now, this is the book I love to read aloud. I love it because the kids love it! Viorst's lead, "She was a pain—a very big pain—in the **b u t t**," hooks young listeners, and her writing magic wins me over. Lulu's strong character and voice shine throughout the novel, making it a perfect mentor text for young writers. If you visit my classroom next year, I'm certain my first graders and I will have yet another must-read chapter book title to share—I can only imagine what it will be!

—*Maria Walther*

Twelve Books Steven Loves to Read Aloud

Narrowing my list to twelve was a horrific experience. I'll start off by saying that I was desperately trying to decide *which* Neal Shusterman book to put on this list when I realized his books had already received, shall I say, more (much more) than their fair share of attention from the classroom teachers' recommendations. So, with respect to Neal, and in consideration of the fact that other people also write great books, I'll say that I echo all Shusterman recommendations heartily. He knows I am a fan.

Can I also tell you my list in this section was originally going to be made up of three titles? Three books. I promise it's true. My thinking was that I had held my invited contributors to only one title, so at most I should do three. It grew to five because I convinced myself that you would be disappointed with three. Three is barely anything substantial. It would be as if you've spent all this time with me—an entire book—and then I leave you with only *three* titles. "It's practically a slap in the face to the readers," I said. *Five*—now, there's a substantial number! Five is something in which I could take great pride. Yes—I quite liked five.

It became ten when the thought occurred to me that it could severely hurt your feelings if I didn't make an effort to cover a wide span of grade levels . . . and genres . . . Don't forget those genres! What an insult to you; I'd be nothing more than a literary hypocrite if I did not make a serious effort to address multiple grade levels and various genres. How could I allow myself to be accused of not practicing what I have preached in my own book? And so, for you, I decided on ten. Ten is good. People expect *ten*, right? Top ten lists. Our entire math system is based on ten (isn't it?). Where's Greg Tang when you need him.

But, you know, the thought struck me, once I had ten, that a lot of people prefer twelve to ten. You know, a dozen of something . . . It just rolls off the tongue, don't you think? A dozen doughnuts, twelve drummers drumming, and all that sort of thing. You see what happened, don't you? And you forgive me because you know that most of you would have done the same thing . . . or worse. So, here they are: twelve favorites, just for you!

"One fine day, from out of town, and without any warning at all, there appeared . . . a magic hat." So opens Mem Fox's masterful picture book about a hat that turns people into animals and restores them to their former selves in the end. Of course, Mem could teach a doctoral-level course with her eyes closed on the subject of word selection and use, rhythm and cadence, and rhyme and word color; she is the master of picture-book writing in my eyes. This book was the favorite of each one of my four children at one point in the early part of their lives. I know, without a doubt, it is the book they will long to read to their own children someday (which is why I have a hardcover copy for each of them when they become parents).

The Magic Hat, for me, has a special quality for oral delivery that sets it in a category all its own. It has a repetitive stanza that any primary teacher knows will lead to choral recitation from the children without so much as a nod or a wink, yet it is not overly re-petitive. I believe the book defies simple categorization: is it a pattern book, a cumulative book, or a storybook? I've heard arguments on all of those fronts, but I'm guessing Mem would tell us she'd prefer that we avoid any discussion of categorization and simply call it a "really great book." So I will.

I'll never forget an undergraduate senior coming up to me about halfway through the semester in my adolescent literature course and practically shrieking, "I can't believe you assigned this book! I would never recommend this book to a teenager!" I wasn't entirely sure what about the title had her so ratcheted up, but upon deep reflection, I settled on the possibility of the main character's father being a serial killer with a large number of teenage boys buried beneath the basement floor as a likely explanation.

Counterfeit Son by Elaine Alphin is my go-to read-aloud for high school kids who need to be enticed back into the experience of being read to by an adult. And it's not really about a serial killer; he gets killed in a shootout in the opening pages. The story is really a compelling psychological thriller that focuses on "the one left behind"—his son, Cameron. When the boy is pulled from the basement by the police, he claims (out of sheer terror) to be one of his father's victims, and a few hours later his "family" comes to take him home. A boy who has never been loved and never known a family is now an imposter—stealing the identity of a boy presumed dead for years. He *is* a counterfeit son . . . or . . . is he?

That student I mentioned before—the one who couldn't believe I assigned the book? Guess who came back to tell me during student teaching that when all else failed to interest her high school class, she decided to read aloud her new *favorite* book. If I have to tell you the title, you need to go back to high school . . . and pay better attention.

Donuthead **by Sue Stauffacher has proven itself to me time and again when it comes to delighting students in the intermediate grades.** Franklin Delano Donuthead is the most neurotic kid I have ever met in a book. He thinks about his own personal safety 24/7! No ladders or trees, no bodies of water, no drinking liquids stored underneath the sink—what a boring kid! He even changes all the smoke detector batteries on a regular schedule.

Franklin's unlikely friendship with a girl who makes Rizzo from *Grease* seem like Shirley Temple is enough to have kids guffawing in no time. Add to that our quirky hero's regular calls to the National Safety Department to report violations (very detailed violations) of safety protocols by teachers and the principal in his elementary school, and you have a recipe for a read-aloud that will reach a fever pitch—especially if you give Franklin a unique "voice" as you perform.

This story is a perfect "light" tale to balance out a heavier coming-of-age book that you might be sharing in these grade levels such as Marion Dane Bauer's fabulous *On My Honor*. (And yes, I realize I just snuck that one in there. And yes, I knew you would notice that I did. And I don't much care, because, really, what are you gonna do about it? The book's already printed, and you don't have the password to get to the electronic version.)

I had a book published in 2001 that never would have been written had it not been for the fact that I was a teacher. During the previous school year a student had dared me in front of an entire class of seventh graders to "write a book for kids like me—kids who hate to read." Foolishly, I announced that I would set to work on that straightaway. (There are relatively few choices at one's disposal when surrounded by a roomful of seventh graders pounding on desks and shouting, "DO IT! DO IT! DO IT!")

When I arrived home after school that night, I was panicked. How was I going to write a novel for kids who hate books? I started by pulling from my bookshelves all the books I had ever read aloud to kids that were titles *everyone* seemed to love and noted their commonalities. They all had intrigue, humor, suspense, cliff-hangers, and a "pinch" of romance. Those became the elements I infused into *This Side of Paradise*—a book that poses disturbing questions. Just how far might a man be willing to go if he was promised the *perfect* family? And what would happen when he eventually reached the terrifying conclusion that in order to attain it, something would first need to be done about the very *imperfect* family he already had?

I read the book aloud over a period of several months, massaging and revising the text based on feedback from kids and colleagues. It went on to receive numerous awards and accolades in the years that followed, but the staying power of the book as a terrific read-aloud has brought me the most joy. I have received letters from teachers of multiple grade levels, letters from teachers in detention centers, and letters from teachers at academies for the gifted—all reassuring me that their kids respond to this read-aloud consistently, year after year, as one of their all-time favorites.

It was not a tough decision for me to include this book in my list, because despite being the author, I can say quite objectively that if I weren't the author, it would still make my list. Why? Because I know what a terrific read-aloud sounds like and feels like in a classroom, and this one hits it out of the ballpark every time.

How can you not fall in love with a picture book about a girl who eats all manner of disgusting things and then throws up—when it's written by a guy whose last name is Grossman? How can that possibly be a coincidence? I've never managed to have my curiosity on that issue satisfied, so I may have to go to the grave still pondering—but if I do, I hope somebody tosses Bill Grossman's *My Little Sister Ate One Hare* into the casket. Those heavenly angels may need me to read them a great picture book once I pass through the pearly gates.

Rhythm and rhyme are put to use in such a way that the story is certain to captivate any audience within minutes. This cumulative tale builds as readers would expect while the narrator's little sister eats, among other things, snakes, polliwogs, and worms as well as shrews and lizards. And she keeps it all down . . . until, that is, she eats some peas. There's nothing like a green vegetable to ruin a kid's good time, and there's nothing like reading aloud this story to engage young readers.

Some people aren't wild about dealing with death—especially in books written for kids. I remember Mrs. Hoochamadoochee coming to one of my colleagues years ago to complain about her reading *Bridge to Terabithia* to the students because "a girl dies in that book, and my child might believe he could die!" News flash, Mrs. H.! By fifth grade I think most of them have already stumbled onto that troublesome piece of reality.

I love the way Barbara Park handles the topic in *Mick Harte Was Here.* First, it's easier on the kids because Mick has already passed away when the book opens. Phoebe, his older and angry sibling, is left to pick up the pieces left by her brother's sudden and entirely unexpected departure. Second, it's raw and realistic. In Phoebe's own words, she hates "my new family of three," and she takes out her hostility over the hand she's been dealt on just about everyone.

What is particularly brilliant of Park and informative to kids is the discovery that Mick lost his life simply by riding his bike with no helmet. The understated accident—

his bike tire just hit a rock in the street and down he came—underscores how easy it is to lose it all. Park's letter to the kids at the end of the book is very convincing—I imagine a lot more of them wearing their bike helmets after hearing this story read aloud. I've always said, "Read-alouds can save lives." Here's a very tangible example.

I was raised in the north, but by a southern woman. It doesn't really matter *where* you are physically being raised when you are being raised by a woman from the South, by the way—you will still hear "that's how we do things in the South" at regular intervals throughout your childhood. My mother and her eight siblings had rural roots, and farming was a way of life for a fair amount of their childhood. My cousins and I have always reveled in their stories of life on the farm, and I believe that may be why Gary Paulsen's *Harris and Me* has been a favorite read-aloud for me for many years. As a matter of fact, I just concluded reading it aloud to my doctoral students a few weeks ago.

This is the book I reach for when I want to generate a discussion about giving voice to characters. I believe I am fairly effective at bringing nine-year-old Harris to life by giving him a voice that I have been told lingers with my students for the rest of their lives. The boy is outrageous to say the least, and his penchant for drawing his visiting cousin, a city boy, into all manner of mayhem provides the perfect backdrop for those who want to introduce students to a character that "stays with you."

Harris does have loose lips in terms of his language; mild profanity marches out on a semiregular basis. This would be unrealistic in some circles, but in a rural area where a nine-year-old boy is unschooled (it appears that way), we wholeheartedly believe it. Humor is one of the two top genres for reaching reluctant readers (mystery is the other), and this book provides it in spades. Moreover, Paulsen masterfully provides two huge and unanticipated moments in the story that, in the words of one of my former eighth graders, "you never see coming."

These are moments of deep reflection—a time to discuss that this is much more than a funny story about a wild boy and his tame cousin. No, this is a story about what it means to belong, to be loved, to have a family. It is one of my favorite examples of powerful writing, and it is made all the more pronounced when we experience it together. A farm isn't typically the place you find a lot of razzle-dazzle, but in the case of this book, there's definitely some read-aloud magic that will happen as soon as you take to the stage.

A few years before I was born, Lloyd Alexander began writing his fabulous Prydain Chronicles. I was not fortunate enough to discover them as a child, but early in my teaching career I was introduced to them, and an indelible mark was left on my heart. I still remember where I was sitting and the emotions flooding over me as I read the final words of the fifth book in the series several years ago. I can say that of no other book.

I teach my graduate students as I taught my elementary and middle schoolers that fantasy books have "different wrapping paper" than other stories. As we peel that unusual wrapping paper back, we must be careful not to become so distracted by its unique attributes that we fail to look at the actual package inside. Readers who are able to accomplish this with Alexander's books are guaranteed to find a treasure. Two of the five books earned Newbery recognition, and the sales figures for the series are astronomical—so somebody agrees with me.

The second book in these chronicles, *The Black Cauldron*, is a particular favorite of mine. The feisty young hero Taran, introduced in the first book along with his intrepid companions, is involved in a mission of heroism, of course, but the lessons he and the readers learn along this particular journey are more powerful than any element or character found in the fantastical land of Prydain. The first book is necessary to lay the groundwork for this one, but the adventure is well worth the time and effort expended to explore this world. I have every intention of reading the entire series again.

Kate DiCamillo's *Because of Winn-Dixie* is nothing short of a masterpiece, and although we usually hear about it being used in the early intermediate grades, I will remind you about "listening up." I'd put it in the early primary grades as a read-aloud and never question the decision. We all know that stories about girls who find puppies are going to tug the heartstrings, and this one surely keeps to that expectation.

Winn-Dixie, however, is not exactly a puppy, nor is he particularly attractive when we first meet him. He grows on us, though, as do many members of Opal's new community. Those who may have been rejected by society are given new life in this loving tale that provides fodder for significant discussion with readers young and old. Miss Gloria, who makes a mean peanut butter sandwich and has liquor bottles hanging from her willow tree to remind her of "someone [she] doesn't ever want to be again," steals my heart every time. She might just grab yours, too, and if she doesn't, then Winn-Dixie's smile is *sure* to do it.

Joan Bauer makes me feel good about the world. I have often said that every book she writes is "a Snuggie and hot cocoa on a cold winter day." When I read a book by Joan, I am forced to curb a sudden impulse to hug people I do not know; I want to throw my beret in the air like Mary Tyler Moore. I believe we all might just "make it after all." In my mind, we could rehabilitate at least 50 percent of all criminals if they were required to read everything Joan Bauer has written and write a self-reflective essay on the experience.

I would have to say that Bauer's *Stand Tall* has moved me to tears every time I've read it aloud. My students saw it; I could never hide it. Fortunately, most of them broke down about the same time I did, so we kept that quiet, along with the secret handshake and the knowledge of who was actually behind all the unexplained technical difficulties that seemed to beleaguer my colleague Mrs. Cawley across the hall in Classroom 113.

The main character, Tree, is a giant not only in physical stature but in his heart. As we suffer the pain of his parents' divorce along with him and learn from the wisdom of his Vietnam veteran grandfather, we find that our hearts are growing as well. The richness of the story has educated every group of students with whom I have shared it. In Chapter 3 of this book, I mentioned that sometimes we read a story aloud simply because it needs to be read aloud—the message is one that desperately needs to be heard. This is that story.

In late 2004, my oldest daughter (who was then two and a half years old) was in crisis. She had a new baby brother who was quite the charmer, and she let us know in short order that she was not joining the fan club! Seared into my memory is the morning she managed to flip him upside down in his baby saucer. The experience led to alarm for him, correction for her, consternation for my wife, and jubilation for me—I got a new book out of it!

Love the Baby was the fastest picture book I have ever written, and it is my favorite picture-book read-aloud. In fact, I can say unequivocally that had I not authored the book, it would *still* be my favorite picture-book read-aloud. In nearly every appearance I make, I am besieged by someone I do not know begging me to read this book aloud during the presentation. Since recording the audio version a few years ago, it has truly taken on a life of its own.

The universality of sibling rivalry appeals to readers of every age, no doubt, but I find it is the building tension that allows me to put my voice to its best use. The combination of just the right words on the page with a finely tuned instrument (my voice) can take the listeners on quite a journey as they experience the fascination, frustration, agitation, and—finally—restoration involved in the tempestuous relationship of these two remarkable bunnies. By the way, in the end, she really did learn to *Love the Baby* . . . after all.

Of all the books I have read aloud to students in my career, it is Jerry Spinelli's *Stargirl* that takes center stage. I read it aloud in elementary school and in middle school, and am now teaching graduate courses at the university and *still* reading it aloud—every year. I do not intend to stop. The story is timeless; the issues it raises always pertinent. The characters make me look harder at myself than characters from any other piece of fiction that I have ever read. I feel like a better person each time I read the final page—and that has to mean something.

In recent years, I've taken to breaking down the last few pages and assigning them to my graduate students to prepare for oral delivery. They practice in advance, and then during our final class, they are able to model some of the techniques I have been teaching them about oral reading as we complete the book together. What they have not discovered, until now, is that the decision to involve them in reading aloud the end of *Stargirl* did not grow out of some impressive form of scaffolded graduate-level instruction; rather, it was born of a combination of necessity and desperation. The truth is, I simply can't read the end out loud without crying. Even after all these years.

In Closing

And now, to my readers, it is time to say good-bye for a while. Until next time . . . take care. Call someone who's not expecting to hear from you. Go last when you could be first. Handwrite your thank-you notes. Read a good book to someone you love. Teach the children—and treat them well.

Keeping the Literacy Lamp Burning,

Steven Layne

REFERENCES

Albright, L. K., and M. Ariail. 2005. "Tapping the Potential of Teacher Read-Alouds in Middle Schools." *Journal of Adolescent and Adult Literacy* 487:582–591.

Allen, J. 2000. *Yellow Brick Roads: Shared and Guided Paths to Independent Reading 4–12.* Portland, ME: Stenhouse.

Anders, P. L., and N. S. Levine. 1990. "Accomplishing Change in Reading Programs." In *Reading in the Middle School,* ed. G. G. Duffy. 2nd ed. Newark, DE: International Reading Association.

Anderson, R. C., E. H. Hiebert, J. A. Scott, and I. A. C. Wilkinson. 1985. *Becoming a Nation of Readers: The Report of the Commission on Reading.* Champaign-Urbana, IL: Center for the Study of Reading.

Ariail, M., and L. K. Albright. 2006. "A Survey of Teachers' Read-Aloud Practices in Middle Schools." *Literacy Research and Instruction* 452:69–89.

Atwell, N. 1998. *In the Middle: New Understandings About Writing, Reading, and Learning.* Portsmouth, NH: Boynton/Cook.

———. 2007. *The Reading Zone.* New York: Scholastic.

Barrs, M., and V. Cork. 2001. *The Reader in the Writer.* London: Centre for Language in Primary Education.

Bauer, M. S., and F. A. Balius, Jr. 1995. "Storytelling: Integrating Therapy and Curriculum for Students with Serious Emotional Disturbances." *Teaching Exceptional Children* 272:24–28.

Beck, I. L., and M. G. McKeown. 2001. "Text Talk: Capturing the Benefits of Read-Aloud Experiences for Young Children." *The Reading Teacher* 551:10–13.

Beers, K. G., and B. Samuels. 1996. *Into Focus: Understanding and Creating Middle School Readers.* Norwood, MA: Christopher Gordon.

Braun, P. 2010. "Taking Time to Read Aloud." *Science Scope* 342:45–49.

Carbo, M. 1996. "Selecting the 'Right' Reading Method." *Teaching Prek–8* 271 (September): 84, 86–87.

Castle, M. 1994. "Helping Children Choose Books." In *Fostering the Love of Reading: The Affective Domain in Reading Education,* ed. E. H. Cramer and M. Castle. Newark, DE: International Reading Association.

Chomsky, C. 1972. "Stages in Language Development and Reading Exposure." *Harvard Educational Review* 421:1–33.

Clay, M. 1979. *Reading: The Patterning of Complex Behavior.* 2nd ed. Auckland, New Zealand: Heinemann.

Cochran-Smith, M. 1984. *The Making of a Reader.* Norwood, NJ: Ablex.

Coiro, J. 2000. "Why Read Aloud?" *Early Childhood Today* 152:12–14.

Combs, M. 1987. "Modeling the Reading Process with Enlarged Texts." *The Reading Teacher* 404:422–426.

Cornell, E. H., M. Senechal, and L. S. Broda. 1988. "Recall of Picture Books by 3-Year-Old Children: Testing and Repetition Effects in Joint Reading Activities." *Journal of Educational Psychology* 804:537–542.

Davidson, J., and D. Koppenhaver. 1993. *Adolescent Literacy: What Works and Why.* New York: Garland.

Delo, L. 2008. "Reading Aloud: Integrating Science and Literature for All Students." *The Science Teacher* 755:33–37.

Donovan, C., E. Milewicz, and L. Smolkin. 2003. "Beyond the Single Text: Nurturing Young Children's Interest in Reading and Writing for Multiple Purposes." *Young Children* 582:30–36.

References

Dorfman, L. R., and R. Cappelli. 2009. *Nonfiction Mentor Texts*. Portland, ME: Stenhouse.

Duchein, M., and D. Mealey. 1993. "Remembrance of Books Past . . . Long Past—Glimpses Into Aliteracy." *Reading Research and Instruction* 331:13–28.

Duke, N. K. 2000. "3.6 Minutes Per Day: The Scarcity of Informational Texts in First Grade." *Reading Research Quarterly* 352:202–224.

Durkin, D. 1974. "A Six-Year Study of Children Who Learned to Read in School at the Age of Four." *Reading Research Quarterly* 101:9–61.

———. 1978. "What Classroom Observations Reveal About Reading Comprehension Instruction." *Reading Research Quarterly* 144:481–533.

———. 1981. "Reading Comprehension Instruction in Five Basal Reading Series." *Reading Research Quarterly* 164:515–544.

Eaton, A. T. 1924. "On Reading Aloud." *The Horn Book* 14:42–46.

Elley, W. B. 1988. *New Vocabulary: How Do Children Learn New Words?* Research and Technical Report No. 143. Wellington, New Zealand: New Zealand Council for Educational Research. ERIC Document Reproduction Service No. ED 298 455.

———. 1989. "Vocabulary Acquisition from Listening to Stories." *Reading Research Quarterly* 242:174–187.

Elley, W. B., and F. Mangubhai. 1983. "The Impact of Reading on Second Language Learning." *Reading Research Quarterly* 191:53–67.

Elster, C. A. 1994. "I Guess They Do Listen: Young Children's Emergent Readings after Adult Read-Alouds." *Young Children* 493:27–31.

Feitelson, D., B. Kita, and Z. Goldstein. 1986. "Effects of Listening to Series Stories on First Graders' Comprehension and Use of Language." *Research in the Teaching of English* 204:339–356.

Ficklen, L., and W. Brooks. 2011. "Reading Aloud to Middle Grade Youth." *Journal of Children's Literature* 371:78–90.

Fisher, D., and N. Frey. 2008. *Improving Adolescent Literacy: Content Area Strategies at Work*. Saddle River, NJ: Pearson.

Forgan, J. W., and A. Gonzalez-DeHass. 2004. "How to Infuse Social Skills Training into Literacy Instruction." *Teaching Exceptional Children* 366:24–30.

Gidlund, D. M. 2011. "Read-Alouds: Impacting Literacy Skills One Book at a Time." *Colorado Reading Council Journal* 22:44–49.

Giorgis, C., N. Johnson, J. Forsburg, and T. DeJong. 2005. "Revisiting Read-Alouds." *Journal of Children's Literature* 311:89–97.

Herrold, W. G. Jr., J. Stanchfield, and A. J. Serabian. 1989. "Comparison of the Effect of a Middle School, Literature-Based Listening Program on Male and Female Attitudes Toward Reading." *Educational Research Quarterly* 134:43–46.

Hicks, K., and B. Wadlington. 1994. "The Efficacy of Shared Reading with Teens." Paper Presented at the Association for Childhood Education International Study Conference, New Orleans, LA, March.

Hoffman, J., N. L. Roser, and J. Battle. 1993. "Reading Aloud in Classrooms: From the Modal Toward a Model." *The Reading Teacher* 466:496–507.

Huck, C. S. 1979. "Literature for All Reasons." *Language Arts* 564:354–355.

Hurst, B., K. Scales, E. Frecks, and K. Lewis. 2011. "Sign Up for Reading: Students Read Aloud to the Class." *The Reading Teacher* 646:439–443.

Irvine, J., and B. Armento. 2001. *Culturally Responsive Teaching: Lesson Planning for Elementary and Middle Grades.* Boston: McGraw Hill.

Ivey, G. 2003. "The Intermediate Grades: The Teacher Makes It More Explainable and Other Reasons to Read Aloud in the Intermediate Grades." *The Reading Teacher* 568:812–814.

Ivey, G., and K. Broaddus. 2001. "Just Plain Reading: A Survey of What Makes Students Want to Read in Middle School Classrooms." *Reading Research Quarterly* 364:350–377.

Jackson, L., and M. V. Panyan. 2002. *Positive Behavioral Support in the Classroom: Principles and Practices.* Baltimore, MD: Paul H. Brookes.

Jennings, J. 1990. "You Can't Afford Not to Read Aloud." *Phi Delta Kappan* 717:568–569.

Kindle, K. 2009. "Vocabulary Development During Read-Alouds: Primary Practices." *The Reading Teacher* 633:202–211.

Kletzien, S. B., and R. Szabo. 1998. "Information Text or Narrative Text? Children's Preferences Revisited." Paper Presented at the National Reading Conference, Austin, TX, December.

Knoth, M. V. 1998. "Reading Aloud to Very Young Children." *Book Links* (July): 22–24.

Kraemer, L., P. McCabe, and R. Sinatra. 2012. "The Effects of Read-Alouds of Expository Text on First Graders' Listening Comprehension and Book Choice." *Literacy Research and Instruction* 512:165–178.

Krashen, S. D. 2004. *The Power of Reading: Insights from the Research*. Westport, CT: Libraries Unlimited.

Labbo, L. D., and W. H. Teale. 1990. "Cross-Age Reading: A Strategy for Helping Poor Readers." *The Reading Teacher* 436:362–369.

Lane, H. B., and T. L. Wright. 2007. "Maximizing the Effectiveness of Reading Aloud." *The Reading Teacher* 607:668–675.

Layne, S. L. 1994. "Read to Your Baby: A Program Designed to Positively Impact the Attitude of Intermediate Readers." *Illinois Reading Council Journal* 222:29–38.

———. 1996. "Vocabulary Acquisition by Fourth-Grade Students from Listening to Teachers' Oral Reading of Novels." Doctoral diss., Northern Illinois University. Retrieved from Proquest Dissertations and Theses Database. Publication No. AAT 9703752.

———. 1998. "Vocabulary Acquisition by Fourth-Grade Students from Listening to Teachers' Oral Reading of Novels." *Illinois Research and Development Journal* 342:16–19.

———. 2009. *Igniting a Passion for Reading*. Portland, ME: Stenhouse.

Lesesne, T. 2003. *Making the Match: The Right Book for the Right Reader at the Right Time, Grades 4–12*. Portland, ME: Stenhouse.

———. 2006. "Reading Aloud: A Worthwhile Investment." *Voices from the Middle* 134:50–54.

Lomax, C. 1976. "Interest in Stories and Books at Nursery School." *Educational Research* 192:100–112.

Maher, E. B. 1991. *The Effect of Reading Aloud to Fifth-Grades Students on the Acquisition of Vocabulary*. Research and Technical Report No. 143. Florida International University. ERIC Document Reproduction Service No. ED 329 904.

McGee, L. M., and J. A. Schickedanz. 2007. "Repeated Interactive Read Alouds in Preschool and Kindergarten." *The Reading Teacher* 608:742–751.

Mokhtari, K., and H. Thompson. 2006. "How Problems of Reading Fluency and Comprehension Are Related to Difficulties in Syntactic Awareness Skills Among Fifth Graders." *Reading Research and Instruction* 461:73–94.

Morgan, H. 2009. "Using Read-Alouds with Culturally Sensitive Children's Books: A Strategy That Can Lead to Tolerance and Improved Reading Skills." *Reading Improvement* 461:3–8.

Morrison, V., and L. Wlodarczyk. 2009. "Revisiting Read-Aloud: Instructional Strategies That Encourage Students' Engagement with Texts." *The Reading Teacher* 632:110–118.

Morrow, L. M. 1983. "Home and School Correlates of Early Interest in Literature." *Journal of Educational Research* 764:221–230.

Morrow, L. M., and J. K. Smith. 1990. "The Effects of Group Size on Interactive Storybook Reading." *Reading Research Quarterly* 253:213–231.

Moss, B. 2008. "The Information Text Gap: The Mismatch Between Non-Narrative Text Types in Basal Readers and 2009 NAEP Recommended Guidelines." *Journal of Literacy Research* 402:201–219.

Ninio, A. 1980. "Picture-Book Reading in Mother-Infant Dyads Belonging to Two Sub-Groups in Israel." *Child Development* 512:587–590.

Ninio, A., and J. Bruner. 1978. "The Achievement and Antecedents of Labeling." *Journal of Child Language* 51:5–15.

Pardeck, J. T. 1990. "Using Bibliotherapy in Clinical Practice with Children." *Psychological Reports* 673:1043–1049.

Paterson, K. 1995. *A Sense of Wonder: On Reading and Writing Books for Children.* New York: Penguin.

Polette, K. 2005. *Read & Write It Out Loud! Guided Oral Literacy Strategies.* Boston: Pearson, Allyn, and Bacon.

Press, M., E. Henenberg, and D. Getman. 2009. "Read-Alouds Move to the Middle Level." *Educator's Voice* 2 (Spring): 36–43.

References

Prus, T. G. 2008. "The Value of Reading Aloud to Learning Disabled Students at the Middle Level." *Wisconsin State Reading Association Journal* 472:13–16.

Richardson, C. C. 1998. "Read-Aloud Time: An Invitation to Dig for Deeper Meaning." *Childhood Education* 651:14–16.

Richardson, J. S. 1981. "Mind Grabbers, or Read Aloud to College Students, Too!" *Ad-Sig Journal* 31:39–51.

———. 1994. "Great Read-Alouds for Prospective Teachers and Secondary Students." *Journal of Reading* 382:98–103.

———. 2000. *Read It Aloud: Using Literature in the Secondary Content Classroom.* Newark, DE: International Reading Association.

Robbins, C., and L. C. Ehri. 1994. "Reading Storybooks to Kindergarteners Helps Them Learn New Vocabulary Words." *Journal of Educational Psychology* 861:54–64.

Robson, C., and S. Whitley. 1989. "Sharing Stories: Parents' Involvement in Reading with Inner-City Nursery Children." *Reading* 231:23–27.

Rosenblatt, L. 1938. *Literature As Exploration.* New York: Modern Language Association.

Roser, N., and M. Martinez. 1985. "Roles Adults Play in Preschoolers' Response to Literature." *Language Arts* 625:485–490.

Routman, R. 1991. *Invitations.* Portsmouth, NH: Heinemann.

———. 2003. *Reading Essentials: The Specifics You Need to Teach Reading Well.* Portsmouth, NH: Heinemann.

Rycik, J. A., and J. L. Irvin. 2005. *Teaching Reading in the Middle Grades: Understanding and Supporting Literacy Development.* Boston: Pearson, Allyn, and Bacon.

Santoro, L., D. Chard, L. Howard, and S. Baker. 2008. "Making the Very Most of Classroom Read-Alouds to Promote Comprehension and Vocabulary." *The Reading Teacher* 615:396–408.

Schickedanz, J. A. 1978. "Please Read That Story Again: Exploring Relationships Between Story Reading and Learning to Read." *Young Children* 335:48–55.

———. 1981. "Hey! This Book Is Not Working Right." *Young Children* 371:18–27.

Shannon, P. 2002. "The Myths of Reading Aloud." *The Dragon Lode* 202:6–11.

Sinatra, R. C. 2008. "Creating a Culture of Vocabulary Acquisition for Children Living in Poverty." *Journal of Children and Poverty* 142:173–192.

Sipe, L. R. 2000. "The Construction of Literary Understanding by First and Second Graders in Oral Response to Picture Storybook Read-Alouds." *Reading Research Quarterly* 352:252–275.

Smolkin, L. B., and C. A. Donovan. 2001. "The Contexts of Comprehension: The Information Book Read-Aloud, Comprehension Acquisition, and Comprehension Instruction in a First-Grade Classroom." *The Elementary School Journal* 1022:97–122.

Snow, C. E., M. S. Burns, and P. Griffin, eds. 1998. *Preventing Reading Difficulties in Young Children.* Washington, DC: National Academy.

Stahl, S. A., M. A. Richek, and R. J. Vandevier. 1990. "Learning Meaning Vocabulary Through Listening: A Sixth-Grade Replication." Paper Presented at the 40th Annual Meeting of the National Reading Conference, Miami, FL, November.

Stead, T. 2014. "Nurturing the Inquiring Mind Through the Nonfiction Read-Aloud." *The Reading Teacher* 677:488–495.

Sticht, T. G., and J. H. James. 1984. "Listening and Reading." In *Handbook of Reading Research,* ed. P. D. Pearson. New York: Longman.

Sullivan, A. K., and H. R. Strang. 2002. "Bibliotherapy in the Classroom: Using Literature to Promote the Development of Emotional Intelligence." *Childhood Education* 792:74–80.

Taylor, D. 1983. *Family Literacy.* Exeter, NH: Heinemann.

Teale, W. H. 2003. "Reading Aloud to Young Children As a Classroom Instructional Activity." In *On Reading Texts to Children: Parents and Teachers,* ed. A. Van Kleeck, S. A. Stahl, and E. B. Bauer. New York: Psychology Press.

Tompkins, G. 2006. *Literacy for the 21st Century: A Balanced Approach.* 4th ed. Upper Saddle River, NJ: Pearson Education.

Trelease, J. 1989. "Jim Trelease Speaks on Reading Aloud to Children." *The Reading Teacher* 433:200–206.

———. 2013. *The Read-Aloud Handbook.* 7th ed. New York: Penguin.

Van Kleeck, A., S. A. Stahl, and E. B. Bauer, eds. 2003. *On Reading Texts to Children: Parents and Teachers.* New York: Psychology Press.

Verden, C. E. 2012. "Reading Culturally Relevant Literature Aloud to Urban Youths with Behavioral Challenges." *Journal of Adolescent and Adult Literacy* 557:619–628.

Wan, G. 2000. "Reading Aloud to Children: The Past, the Present, the Future." *Reading Improvement* 37:148–160.

Warren, J. S., N. J. Prater, and D. L. Griswold. 1990. "Parental Practices of Reading Aloud to Preschool Children." *Reading Improvement* 271:41–45.

Wiesendanger, K., and L. Bader. 1989. "Children's View of Motivation." *The Reading Teacher* 424:345–347.

Wilson, E. A. 1999. *Reading at the Middle and High School Levels: Building Active Readers Across the Curriculum.* 2nd ed. Arlington, VA: Educational Research Service.

Worthy, J., K. Chamberlain, K. Peterson, C. Sharp, and P. Shih. 2012. "The Importance of Read Aloud and Dialogue in an Era of Narrowed Curriculum: An Examination of Literature Discussions in a Second-Grade Classroom." *Literacy Research and Instruction* 514:308–321.

Yaden, D. B. 1988. "Understanding Stories Through Repeated Read-Alouds: How Many Does It Take?" *The Reading Teacher* 416:556–560.

Yaden, D. B., L. B. Smolkin, and A. Conlon. 1989. "Preschoolers' Questions About Pictures, Print Conventions, and Story Text During Reading Aloud at Home." *Reading Research Quarterly* 242:188–213.

Yopp, R. H., and H. K. Yopp. 2006. "Information Texts as Read-Alouds at School and Home." *Journal of Literacy Research* 381:37–51.

Zehr, M. 2010. "Reading Aloud to Teens Gains Favor." *Education Week* 2916:1–13.

Children's and Young Adult Books

Alexander L. 1964. *The Book of Three.* New York: Dell.

———. 1965. *The Black Cauldron.* New York: Dell.

Alphin, E. M. 2000. *Counterfeit Son.* New York: Harcourt.

Andreae, G. 2012. *Giraffes Can't Dance.* New York: Scholastic.

Atwater, R., and F. Atwater. 1938. *Mr. Popper's Penguins.* Boston: Little, Brown.

Avi. 1990. *The True Confessions of Charlotte Doyle.* New York: Avon.

Bauer, J. 1998. *Rules of the Road.* New York: Penguin.

———. 2000. *Hope Was Here.* New York: Penguin.

———. 2002. *Stand Tall.* New York: Penguin.

Bauer, M. D. 1986. *On My Honor.* New York: Random House.

Baylor, B. 1974. *Everybody Needs a Rock.* New York: Simon and Schuster.

Beah, I. 2007. *A Long Way Gone: Memoirs of a Boy Soldier.* New York: Farrar, Straus and Giroux.

Beamer, L. 2002. *Let's Roll! Ordinary People, Extraordinary Courage.* Wheaton, IL: Tyndale.

Beatty, P. 1999. *Turn Homeward, Hannalee.* New York: HarperCollins.

Beaumont, K. 2005. *I Ain't Gonna Paint No More!* New York: Harcourt.

———. 2008. *Who Ate All the Cookie Dough?* New York: Henry Holt.

Berger, M., and G. Berger. 2009. *True or False: Dangerous Animals.* New York: Scholastic.

Birdsall, J. 2005. *The Penderwicks.* New York: Knopf.

Birney, B. 2005. *The World According to Humphrey.* New York: Penguin.

Bishop, N. 2012. *Snakes.* New York: Scholastic.

Bradby, M. 1995. *More Than Anything Else.* New York: Scholastic.

Buckley, C. 2009. *Tarra and Bella: The Elephant and Dog Who Became Friends.* New York: Penguin.

Burch, J. M. 1985. *They Cage the Animals at Night.* New York: Penguin.

References

Carroll, L. 2004. *Jabberwocky.* Tonawanda, NY: Kids Can Press.

Casanova, M. 2003. *One-Dog Canoe.* New York: Farrar, Straus and Giroux.

Clavell, J. 1963. *The Children's Story.* New York: Dell.

Cleary, B. 1955. *Beezus and Ramona.* New York: William Morrow.

Clements, A. 1998. *Frindle.* New York: Atheneum.

Coelho, P. 1988. *The Alchemist.* New York: HarperCollins.

Collins, S. 2003. *Gregor the Overlander.* New York: Scholastic.

———. 2008. *The Hunger Games.* New York: Scholastic.

Cooney, B. 1982. *Miss Rumphius.* New York: Penguin.

Covey, S. 2006. *The 6 Most Important Decisions You'll Ever Make: A Guide for Teens.* New York: Simon and Schuster.

Coy, J. 2013. *Hoop Genius: How a Desperate Teacher and a Rowdy Gym Class Invented Basketball.* Minneapolis, MN: Lerner.

Dahl, R. 1982. *The BFG.* New York: Puffin.

———. 1988. *James and the Giant Peach.* New York: Puffin.

Daywalt, D. 2013. *The Day the Crayons Quit.* New York: Philomel.

DiCamillo, K. 2000. *Because of Winn-Dixie.* Cambridge, MA: Candlewick.

———. 2003. *The Tale of Despereaux.* Cambridge, MA: Candlewick.

———. 2006. *The Miraculous Journey of Edward Tulane.* Cambridge, MA: Candlewick.

Dickens, C. 1860. *Great Expectations.* New York: Penguin.

Draper, S. 2010. *Out of My Mind.* New York: Atheneum.

Dumas, F. 2004. *Funny in Farsi: A Memoir of Growing Up Iranian in America.* New York: Random House.

Eagleman, D. 2010. *Sum: Forty Tales from the After Lives.* New York: Knopf.

Earl, E. 2014. *This Star Won't Go Out: The Life and Words of Esther Grace Earl.* New York: Penguin.

Edmonds, W. 1941. *The Matchlock Gun.* New York: Penguin.

Ehlert, L. 2014. *The Scraps Book: Notes from a Colorful Life.* New York: Simon and Schuster.

Finkel, D. 2009. *The Good Soldiers.* New York: Farrar, Straus and Giroux.

Floca, B. 2013. *Locomotive.* New York: Atheneum.

Fox, M. 1988. *Koala Lou.* New York: Harcourt.

———. 2002. *The Magic Hat.* New York: Harcourt.

Garcia, L. 2005. *The Legend of the Wandering King.* New York: Scholastic.

Giovanni, N. 1973. *Ego-Tripping and Other Poems for Young People.* Chicago, IL: Chicago Review Press.

Golding, W. 1954. *Lord of the Flies.* New York: Penguin.

Goldman, W. 2007. *The Princess Bride.* New York: Harcourt.

Green, J. 2012. *The Fault in Our Stars.* New York: Penguin.

Grossman, B. 1998. *My Little Sister Ate One Hare.* New York: Crown.

Haney, E. L. 2002. *Inside Delta Force.* New York: Dell.

Haseley, D. 2002. *A Story for Bear.* New York: Harcourt.

Henkes, K. 1996. *Lilly's Purple Plastic Purse.* New York: Greenwillow.

Holbrook, S. 1998. *Chicks Up Front.* Cleveland, OH: Cleveland State University Poetry Center.

Jenkins, S. 2004. *Actual Size.* Boston: Houghton Mifflin.

Kalman, M. 2002. *Fireboat: The Heroic Adventures of the John J. Harvey.* New York: Penguin.

Korman, G. 2012. *Ungifted.* New York: HarperCollins.

Kwaymullina, A. 2014. *The Interrogation of Ashala Wolf.* Cambridge, MA: Candlewick.

Lai, T. 2013. *Inside Out and Back Again.* New York: HarperCollins.

LaRochelle, D. 2004. *The Best Pet of All.* New York: Penguin.

Layne, S. 2001. *This Side of Paradise.* Gretna, LA: Pelican.

———. 2007. *Love the Baby.* Gretna, LA: Pelican.

Lee, Harper. 1960. *To Kill a Mockingbird.* Philadelphia: HarperCollins.

References

L'Engle, M. 1962. *A Wrinkle in Time.* New York: Dell.

Levine, E. 2007. *Henry's Freedom Box.* New York: Scholastic

Lewis, C. S. 1950. *The Lion, the Witch, and the Wardrobe.* New York: HarperCollins.

Lindgren, A. 1950. *Pippi Longstocking.* New York: Penguin.

Lowry, L. 1988. *All About Sam.* New York: Random House.

———. 1993. *The Giver.* New York: Dell.

———. 2002. *Gooney Bird Greene.* New York: Random House.

MacDonald, B. 1947. *Mrs. Piggle Wiggle.* New York: HarperCollins.

MacLachlan, P. 1994. *All the Places to Love.* New York: Harcourt.

Mazer, A. 1991. *The Salamander Room.* New York: Knopf.

McDonald, M. 2005. *Stink: The Incredible Shrinking Kid.* Somerville, MA: Candlewick.

Merriam, E. 1991. *The Wise Woman and Her Secret.* New York: Simon and Schuster.

Mewburn, K. 2008. *Kiss! Kiss! Yuck! Yuck!* Atlanta, GA: Peachtree.

Mikaelsen, B. 2001. *Touching Spirit Bear.* New York: HarperCollins.

Mowat, F. 1961. *Owls in the Family.* Toronto, ON: McClelland and Stewart.

Murphy, J. 1995. *The Great Fire.* New York: Scholastic.

Nancy, T. L. 1997. *Letters from a Nut.* New York: Scholastic.

Nelson, P. 2002. *Left for Dead: A Young Man's Search for Justice for the USS* Indianapolis. New York: Random House.

Nemat, M. 2008. *Prisoner of Tehran.* New York: Simon and Schuster.

O'Connor, J. 2005. *Fancy Nancy.* New York: HarperCollins.

O'Dell, S. 1960. *Island of the Blue Dolphins.* New York: Dell.

Park, B. 1982. *Skinnybones.* New York: Random House.

———. 1987. *The Kid in the Red Jacket.* New York: Dell.

———. 1995. *Mick Harte Was Here.* New York: Random House.

———. 2001. *Junie B. Jones Is a Graduation Girl.* New York: Random House.

Paterson, K. 1987. *Bridge to Terabithia*. New York: HarperCollins.

Paulsen, G. 1993. *Harris and Me*. New York: Dell.

———. 2003. *How Angel Peterson Got His Name*. New York: Random House.

Pausch, R. 2008. *The Last Lecture*. New York: Hyperion.

Philbrick, R. 2000. *The Last Book in the Universe*. New York: Scholastic.

Pinborough, J. 2013. *Miss Moore Thought Otherwise*. New York: Houghton Mifflin.

Roberts, W. D. 2004. *Blood on His Hands*. New York: Atheneum.

Rusch, E. 2013. *Electrical Wizard: How Nikola Tesla Lit Up the World*. Cambridge, MA: Candlewick.

Schwartz, A. 1989. *Scary Stories to Tell in the Dark*. New York: HarperCollins.

Selznick, B. 2007. *The Invention of Hugo Cabret*. New York: Scholastic.

Sendak, M. 1963. *Where the Wild Things Are*. New York: HarperCollins.

Shafer, A. 2008. *The Mailbox*. New York: Random House.

Sheinkin, S. 2012. *Bomb: The Race to Build—and Steal—the World's Most Dangerous Weapon*. New York: Roaring Brook.

———. 2012. *Lincoln's Grave Robbers*. New York: Scholastic.

Shusterman, N. 1988. *The Shadow Club*. New York: Dell.

———. 2004. *The Schwa Was Here*. New York: Penguin.

———. 2007. *Unwind*. New York: Simon and Schuster.

———. 2010. *Bruiser*. New York: HarperCollins.

Sonnenblick, J. 2008. *Dodger and Me*. New York: Macmillan.

Spinelli, J. 2000. *Stargirl*. New York: Knopf.

Staples, S. F. 1989. *Shabanu: Daughter of the Wind*. New York: Random House.

Stauffacher, S. 2003. *Donuthead*. New York: Random House.

Stead, R. 2009. *When You Reach Me*. New York: Random House.

Teague, M. 2002. *Dear Mrs. LaRue: Letters from Obedience School*. New York: Scholastic.

References

Thiele, C. 2007. *The Fiery Salamander*. Sydney, Australia: Hachette.

Tobias, T. 2000. *Serendipity*. New York: Simon and Schuster.

Truss, L. 2008. *Twenty-Odd Ducks: Why Every Punctuation Mark Counts!* New York: Penguin.

Van Allsburg, C. 1985. *The Polar Express*. New York: Houghton Mifflin.

Viorst, J. 2012. *Lulu and the Brontosaurus*. New York: Atheneum.

Walker, S. M. 1998. *The 18 Penny Goose*. New York: HarperCollins.

———. 2011. *Blizzard of Glass: The Halifax Explosion of 1917*. New York: Henry Holt.

Watt, M. 2006. *Scaredy Squirrel*. New York: Kids Can Press.

———. 2009. *Have I Got a Book for You*. New York: Kids Can Press.

Werlin, N. 2006. *The Rules of Survival*. New York: Dial.

White, E. B. 1945. *Stuart Little*. New York: HarperCollins.

———. 1952. *Charlotte's Web*. New York: HarperCollins.

Wild, M. 2006. *Fox*. Melbourne, Australia: Allen and Unwin.

Wilder, L. I. 1953. *Little House in the Big Woods*. New York: HarperCollins.

Wilson, K. 2006. *Moose Tracks*. New York: Simon and Schuster.

Wolf, A. 2011. *The Watch That Ends the Night*. Somerville, MA: Candlewick.

Woodson, J. 2001. *The Other Side*. New York: Penguin.

———. 2005. *Show Way*. New York: Penguin.

INDEX

writing process, 4, 22
 emotional truth, 52–53
 experience and, 80–81, 100, 102
 reflection and, 101
 research and, 101

Y

Young, Courtney L., 124
young adult literature, social issues, 50–52

Z

Zulauf, Ben, 110